a SAVOR THE SOUTH *cookbook*

Rice

SAVOR THE SOUTH *cookbooks*

Pie, by Sara Foster (2018)
Ham, by Damon Lee Fowler (2017)
Corn, by Tema Flanagan (2017)
Fruit, by Nancie McDermott (2017)
Chicken, by Cynthia Graubart (2016)
Bacon, by Fred Thompson (2016)
Greens, by Thomas Head (2016)
Barbecue, by John Shelton Reed (2016)
Crabs and Oysters, by Bill Smith (2015)
Sunday Dinner, by Bridgette A. Lacy (2015)
Beans and Field Peas, by Sandra A. Gutierrez (2015)
Gumbo, by Dale Curry (2015)
Shrimp, by Jay Pierce (2015)
Catfish, by Paul and Angela Knipple (2015)
Sweet Potatoes, by April McGreger (2014)
Southern Holidays, by Debbie Moose (2014)
Okra, by Virginia Willis (2014)
Pickles and Preserves, by Andrea Weigl (2014)
Bourbon, by Kathleen Purvis (2013)
Biscuits, by Belinda Ellis (2013)
Tomatoes, by Miriam Rubin (2013)
Peaches, by Kelly Alexander (2013)
Pecans, by Kathleen Purvis (2012)
Buttermilk, by Debbie Moose (2012)

a SAVOR THE SOUTH *cookbook*

Rice

MICHAEL W. TWITTY

The University of North Carolina Press CHAPEL HILL

The University of North Carolina Press has been a member
of the Green Press Initiative since 2003.

Cover photo © iStock/SvetlanaK

Library of Congress Cataloging-in-Publication Data
Names: Twitty, Michael, 1977– author.
Title: Rice / Michael W. Twitty.
Other titles: Savor the South cookbook.
Description: Chapel Hill : The University of North Carolina Press, [2021] |
Series: A savor the South cookbook | Includes index.
Identifiers: LCCN 2020044099 | ISBN 9781469660240 (cloth) |
ISBN 9781469660257 (ebook)
Subjects: LCSH: Cooking (Rice) | Cooking, American—Southern style. |
International cooking. | LCGFT: Cookbooks.
Classification: LCC TX809.R5 T85 2021 | DDC 641.6/318—dc23
LC record available at https://lccn.loc.gov/2020044099

For Mama and Grammy, and for their
ancient mothers, my ancestors from Sierra Leone

Contents

a SAVOR THE SOUTH *cookbook*

Rice

Introduction

f the three grains that dominate the southern table—corn, wheat, and rice—rice is without question the most versatile. To southerners, rice is welcome at breakfast, lunch, and dinner; it works as a main dish, side dish, or snack. There's a good reason for that: it's filling, it's delicious when properly prepared, and its texture and mouthfeel vary depending on the recipe; in some dishes it is crunchingly crispy, in others, soothingly smooth—and there's a whole range of satisfying possibilities in between. Rice has textures, scents, tastes, and depths of flavor that make it indispensable to the cuisines of the South, from Creole and Acadian foodways to soul food to the foodways of the Low Country and Gulf Coast and the ethnic communities that have populated the region since its earliest days.

While rice has its own intrinsic grandeur—connoisseurs can tell the difference between thousands of varieties—it's how rice dances with other foods at the feast that really counts to many cooks and eaters. Tomatoes plus rice, for example, equals umami pop, a rich, savory satisfaction rivaled only by the play of texture, flavor, and scent that is rice and onions. Or what about the moment when rice, paired simply with chicken, absorbs those globules of fat and jus? Rice and peas are not starch on starch; they're two flavor sponges side by side, soaking up all the energy of the dance. My favorite rice dishes are the ones that make you feel full, satisfied, and hungry for leftovers, like red rice, whose tomato, onion, and meaty taste make it my queen of all Southern dishes. But just flip the script to go with sweet instead of savory and you have rice pudding, a dessert dish so good you're willing to burn your mouth to taste it.

Rice's perfume marries well with the scent of other ingredients and amplifies what we like most about rice: it changes outfits well to suit the party. When we pair it with sugar, vanilla, cinnamon, and other fragrant elements, rice reminds us how creamy and neutralizing it can be.

Rice is unique as an ingredient, with an architecture that bids us to build a recipe that keeps its taste and texture at the center. Rice can be red, reddish-orange, green, yellow, black, or white. It has an unforgettable desire attached to it, and nostalgia and locality contribute to its longevity. Rice dishes, whether sweet, spicy, hot, cold, oniony, salty, or creamy, are the go-to food for many of us when we seek comfort. For many of us southerners, no other ingredient tastes this much like home.

At the same time, rice is absolutely a global food. It's a staple of infinite variety, and its history weaves in and out of the global story that is southern culture. From enslaved people from West Africa, to Vietnamese and Kurdish refugees, to Canary Islanders and Italians, those who brought rice dishes from their homelands with them to the South also embodied narratives laden with struggle and survival, migration, movement, and family tradition. Rice also bonds the Lower South with much of the rest of the planet, for whom a meal without rice is, frankly, not a meal at all.

Southern rice tells a bigger and richer story than many of its sister grains and dishes, though all are uniquely cherished. Corn tells how a Native American staple went from versatile fare to a food with limited notes. Wheat is part of the tale of European colonization, with bread being central to the spiritual and economic life of western European settlers. Rice, on the other hand, is where Africa and Asia come in. Unlike its sisters, rice for many southerners engenders very sharp feelings of nostalgia and food memory. Rice with butter and sugar often pushes grits aside in the morning, bread made with rice can rival dinner rolls and cornbread, and rice pudding gives cake and pie a run for their money.

And we haven't even gotten to the part where rice makes its appearance across the entire table, from soup (it's a must in gumbo) to side dish (have you tried crab rice?) to main dish (jambalaya, a rival of risotto and pilau) to nuts (pecan-studded rice).

My Own Story

Rice has played a pivotal role in shaping my identity. My favorite rice dish growing up was my Alabama-born grandmother's red rice (often misnamed "Spanish rice"), a tasty, tomato-rich rice pilau with bell peppers, onions, and spices. Little did I know then that if you followed that one dish back through all of the mamas and grandmas that came before her, you would go overland from Alabama to South Carolina and then across the Atlantic. My grandmother's great-grandmother was born in Charleston, the center of red rice country, and *her* great-grandmother's grandmother was born in Sierra Leone, among the Mende people. To this day, one of the staple dishes of Sierra Leone is jollof rice, the West African antecedent of red rice. Prepared in different ways up and down the Atlantic world rice belt, today's versions of red rice essentially maintain the same orange-red glow, as well as a taste that is pleasantly warm and pairs well with just about any leafy green or protein.

As a culinary historian and historic interpreter, I am never happier than when I've got in front of me a solid dish of red rice. This simple, hearty dish—one of the many direct contributions of West Africa to the southern table—isn't only an edible link to my genes, my DNA, blood, and bone. It's a way to my heart. They say in Sierra Leone that if you have not eaten rice that day, then you haven't really eaten at all. I appreciate that sentiment, as fare like pilau (in some places called perloo), a simple southern chicken-and-rice dish, or a rice crepe stuffed with green onions, Vietnamese herbs, and fresh seafood, triggers some of my most Pavlovian moments.

But even more important, rice connects me to every other person, southern and global, who is nourished by rice's traditions and customs.

A Grain of the Global South

There's an apocryphal story that rice entered the South through Charleston in 1685. A ship blown off its course from Madagascar to England landed unexpectedly in Charleston, where aid was provided to the crew. The grateful captain repaid the colonial British governor's hospitality with seed grains from rice, which from then on could be grown in Carolina and used to enrich the colony for all time.

Though rice most likely was already here when the ship from Madagascar arrived, this story of rice's entrance into the South highlights how significant it was for the region. In the antebellum South, if cotton was the king of commodities, then rice was the queen. And the queen bought incomparable economic power. Charleston and, later, Savannah were thriving cosmopolitan trading ports, with fabulous wealth guaranteed by the cultivation of cash crops, which relied on the knowledge and labor of enslaved West and Central Africans.

West Africans from Senegal to Liberia, the western half of Cote d'Ivoire (the Ivory Coast), and deep into the interior along the Niger and other rivers, had grown rice for almost four millennia by the time the transatlantic slave trade picked up in earnest. With the spread of Islam and the settlement of the western African coastline by the Portuguese, the indigenous African red rice known as *Oryza glaberrima* and several other wild and cultivated species were joined by *Oryza sativa*, or "Asian rice." On the island of Madagascar, some of my other ancestors were growing the latter, their ancestors having brought seed from Indonesia in outrigger canoes. As African and Asian cultures mixed, rice became both a staple and the central feature of Madagascan economic life. In West Africa, too, my forebears knew this reality, with women taking a primary role in processing of the crop.

It's no accident that my grandmothers passed their knowledge of rice culture from generation to generation. From 1750 to 1775, planters from southeastern North Carolina through South Carolina and Georgia to northeastern Florida imported thousands of enslaved human beings, many of them women, to properly grow and process husked rice. The Mende, Temne, Sherbro, Manjack, Balanta, Papel, Kru, Vai, Kissi, Grebo, Bassari, Limba, and many other ethnic groups were already rice-production experts, and in Africa, once their rice was grown, they processed it with incredibly beautiful winnowing baskets and expertly carved standing mortars and pestles that, in the right hands, produced thousands of tons of polished, unbroken rice.

From this period in the eighteenth century came the inflorescence of what historian Karen Hess famously called "the rice kitchen." Southern rice dishes were based on West African precedent: rice was steamed, with each grain separate and distinct, and paired with soups, stews, heavy sauces, and fried or grilled proteins.

On the other side of the South—along the Gulf Coast and up the Mississippi River valley—Africans were sent, carrying rice that had originated in Benin and Senegal, to develop the Louisiana colony and environs in the 1720s. While the Low Country experienced its own rice boom, rice in the Louisiana area became a staple thanks to ethnic groups from Senegambia, including the Bamana, Serer, Diola, Fula, and Malinke, who made up roughly two-thirds of the African people who were imported through the French trade. Other Africans arrived with similar knowledge because they grew Asian rice to supplement supplies on slave ships sent to the Americas. During the French colonization of Louisiana, in Creole cuisine, and later an amended Acadian (or Cajun) cuisine, rice took a central role—in contrast to its status as a luxury food in most of France at the time. Piping-hot rice fritters, red beans and rice made by Haitian émigrés, gumbos with bowls of rice, and a wealth of variations on rice breads, mushes, dressings, and pilaus poured out of Louisiana kitchens high and low.

In the American colonies, and, of course, after the American Revolution as well, these African experts in rice cultivation were forced to work under the lash in an environment featuring new germs, relentless insects, and intense heat and cold. Rice fields took many lives as malaria and yellow fever plagued the "street," the Low Country term for enslaved people's living quarters. It was so bad that one-quarter of all Africans arriving in North America went to Charleston, many to make up for earlier losses of life in the marshes where rice was grown. Slaveholders, on the other hand, often had two residences: one in the country for the winter months and one in the city for the summer, when insect-borne diseases were at their height. Rice, for all the joy and nourishment it has given, was part of a system that created inequality for generations.

Enslaved people, poor whites, and Native Americans lived together or in close proximity in early southern communities, and rice was consumed across their diets. The typical one-pot meal might have been cooked in colonoware, a type of earthenware created by African Americans along the Atlantic coast and westward. Or it might have been cooked in a cast-iron pot or Dutch oven. Such preparations helped rice-based dishes become practical and popular. Their rice was often the broken, cheaper castoffs. But no matter: rice grits blended well into mixtures of seasonal vegetables, herbs, and spices, along with whatever protein was available, and rice cakes and fritters were made with leftovers. In some ways, rice was kind of a southern manna.

It's not an accident that South Carolina, Georgia, Florida, and Louisiana produced two of the most African-centered food cultures and folk cultures in America: the Gullah-Geechee people of the Low Country coast and Sea Islands, and the Creoles of African descent in the Gulf region and Lower Mississippi River valley. Rice went hand in hand with new words for dishes born in New World slavery, just as it went hand in hand with the music, religion, dance, and Afri-Creole languages that created new American cultures. But what was most impressive is that these cultures didn't exist in a bubble; they influenced everyone around them and have had a lasting impact on all of southern culture.

We can see the importance of rice in African American folklore, which carried over rice's unique mythology from Africa. Supposedly carried in seed form in the braided hair of African grandmothers, rice offered the enslaved a hidden and sacred link to ancestors and their deities. Among my Mende forebears, for instance, rice mixed with palm oil fed the ancestors at their graves. For many other groups, too, African rice was a revered food, not just dinner. According to Newbell Niles Puckett, a folklorist who worked at the turn of the twentieth century, many of these customs endured, empowered by thousands of years of songs, prayers, and recipes. All of this experience, all of these stories, have enriched the southern embrace of rice, right down to the custom of eating rice with black-eyed peas on New Year's Day.

Rice marched across the South in the hands of the enslaved and enslavers. It was not only a plantation crop, and it was not grown solely in hot, swampy parts of the southeastern coast. In the present day of agricultural monotony, it's easy to forget that there are *thousands* of varieties of *Oryza sativa,* many of them cultivated in the past. Each variety has significant, specific growing requirements, and some are quite amenable to colder or drier climates. Historian David Shields and others have shown that rice was grown in small home plots across the South in places that would surprise us today—from the North Carolina Piedmont to the Eastern Shore of Maryland to the middle of Tennessee. The rice patch, along with the cornfield, sustained many southern homesteads even into the Great Depression.

Today, rice—in its many incarnations and forms—is one of the most popular foods across the South and, indeed, across the nation. As a cash crop, however, rice was badly hurt by hurricanes at the end of the nineteenth century, especially a particularly devastating storm in 1911. Since then, rice has recovered and now is among the top ten produce crops grown in the United States, almost exclusively in the South and California, with approximately half of rice sales by volume going to global markets.

Southern Varieties

Many types of rice have graced southern tables, from Carolina White to Carolina Gold, from basmati to jasmine, from short to medium to long grain. Here, I look at some of these varieties more closely, as they are tied in intricate and rich ways to southern culture.

The original African red rice persists in southern lowlands. While it has commonly been viewed as an invasive species, recently it has been experiencing a celebratory boost as an effort to recover several varieties of African rice is underway. This effort is being led by the descendants of enslaved people on Low Country plantations who, during the War of 1812, escaped with the British soldiers from Gullah-Geechee communities to Trinidad. But long before this effort to recover the original African rice, Thomas Jefferson had been keen to expand rice cultivation during the Revolutionary era, when he smuggled, on pain of death, Arborio rice from the Po Valley in Italy to his Virginia plantation. He also acquired rice from the highlands of upper Guinea, a variety that would eventually come to be grown across the South on homesteads. Indeed, this variety gained importance as a secondary staple among escaped enslaved Africans, and Creek, Choctaw, and Seminole Indians, all of whom grew patches of "home rice."

The history of southern varieties shifted after the end of slavery and after a series of destructive hurricanes at the beginning of the twentieth century. Rice production grew in Louisiana, Mississippi, Arkansas, Missouri, Texas, and, later, California. Texas boasted basmati varieties developed for its eastern region: Teximati is perfect for true Texas chili con carne. But rice grown on homesteads had died out for the most part by World War II. The thumping, rhythmic sound of rice being husked and the songs and beats that went with that laborious activity ceased, and bags of non-local rice filled the family larders. Apart from Louisiana and Texas, in the South, rice was no longer a homegrown, local crop for most southerners, even as they continued to love eating rice.

Today, I'm glad to report one success story in the realm of local varieties of rice: Carolina Gold, the queen among queens. Named for its beautiful husk, Carolina Gold rice was the original variety that turned many Low Country planters into some of the wealthiest men and women in American history, including one Joshua John Ward, who held in bondage vast numbers of enslaved people. Carolina Gold's cultivation fueled an early rice industry that exported millions of pounds of rice to other locations in the Americas and to Europe.

The cultivation of Carolina Gold was revived in the 1980s when a judge who liked to hunt ducks was looking for his prey among its favorite food. Through the efforts of Glenn Roberts and the Carolina Gold Rice Foundation, founded in 1988, acreage of the crop has expanded, and now Carolina Gold is cooked by outstanding chefs in many southern restaurants and by others who appreciate it as an important ingredient with a story and taste worth preserving.

I gathered some excellent tips about cooking Carolina Gold from Chef BJ Dennis, a renowned Gullah-Geechee chef born and raised in Charleston, and I pass them along here. It is best to wash Carolina Gold three or four times before you cook it. If you choose not to wash it, you should partially steam it for ten to fifteen minutes in order to neutralize the starch, so you can avoid very sticky cooked rice. For cooking, the water-to-rice ratio is 1 to 1. If you have broken rice to cook, however, the water-to-rice ration is about ¾ to 1. A Dutch oven is the best pot for cooking Carolina Gold.

Another traditional variety, the upland rice known as Merikin, is on the verge of the same rebirth. With the engagement of the southern Gullah-Geechee community, encouraged by the work of ethnobotanist Dr. Francis Morean of Trinidad and Tobago, Merikin is being grown as a new crop in the Low Country.

Rice Dances with Everything

Part of the magic of rice is the way it expands in size, as well as how it transforms from hard and inedible to soft and malleable. Rice is also incredibly flexible. It can be eaten on its own or tossed into a salad, soup, or main dish to provide body and volume. As with fried rice or rice and gravy, rice can make a complete meal with leftovers and bits from the pan. In the past, rice was often used to bulk up bread and other baked goods, and rice offered quick, frugal solutions for breakfast and dessert when self-reliance and thriftiness were key to survival. Rice dishes were easy ways to stretch a budget and feed a crowd.

Let me contemplate here one type of southern rice dish—pilau—that illuminates the southern culture of self-reliance and thriftiness, and show how it connects the vastly diverse region that we call the South. If we were to take a tour of the rice dishes of the South, we would quickly see that West African, Middle

Eastern, Indian, and Spanish dishes, and many other cultures' cuisines that have been influenced by them, form an important category called pilaus, seasoned rice cooked in stock, often with other ingredients. If you were to speak to recent immigrants to the South from parts of Central Asia, they would readily recognize the term "pilau" because plov, a one-plate rice dish, is a staple there. The South has always had its own way of putting unique spins on names, and somehow "pilau" came to be pronounced "perloo" in the Low Country. There are many, many pilaus; red rice, for example, is the same thing as "tomato pilau." A changing cast of main ingredients—okra, shrimp, oysters, crab, greens—take turns in regional or local pilaus.

The family tree of southern rice dishes gets very fuzzy when we talk about pilau. The influences of the French court and French and Spanish foodways were refracted through an African lens in the Low Country, Lower Mississippi Valley, and Gulf Coast. We know that a ship bearing enslaved people familiar with rice cultivation anchored at different times at different southern ports, and the local pilau reflected what was seasonally available. While Charleston pilau, which often featured chicken, shrimp, and sausage, and New Orleans jambalaya have very similar ingredients—rice, tomatoes, onions, bell peppers, and the protein of your choice—pilaus extending into landlocked middle Georgia featured country sausage. In Florida, chicken-and-rice pilaus were a celebration mainstay—rice and a few spices were cooked in the water used for boiling a chicken, and the meat was then shredded and added back to the humongous pot. We also see Native American influences in some pilaus, and it would be fascinating to do deeper research in this area of American foodways.

Bean pilaus further complicate the culinary network among Louisiana and Low Country rice kitchens. Jambalaya au congri is pretty much the same dish as Hoppin' John. Both go back to colonial days, when enslaved people brought their rice cuisine with them from Africa in a major way, not so much in their hair but in their minds. Jambalaya au congri calls for black-eyed peas and other pale cowpeas, but Hoppin' John was appreciated for its use of the Sea Island red pea. Other Hoppin' John–like dishes across the South utilize black-eyed peas or other local cowpeas. All make their premier appearance on New Year's Day to bring good luck for the rest of the year.

Red beans and rice, which can be considered part of the pilau family, is known as "the Monday dish" because Monday was traditionally laundry day from the early nineteenth to the mid-twentieth century and it was an easy dish to set and forget in a pot on the other side of the kitchen and laundry site. Red beans and rice has an African culinary history. In Senegal and Gambia, the tradition of eating ceebu niebe—rice and cowpeas—was well known. Rice and beans was a staple all over West Africa, as it is to this day. Haiti, from which many émigrés came to the United States in the 1790s and early 1800s, was deeply connected to African cultural and culinary roots. Black Haitians, who integrated among their Creole cousins in New Orleans, were responsible for seeding this signature dish, yet another variation on the idea of a pilau, in Louisiana.

Rice cooked so that each grain is separate and distinct is a critical part of another sort of southern dish. Charleston's answer to curry, country captain, depends on a steaming plate of fragrant, fresh Carolina Gold, just as okra, oysters, sesame—another ingredient with an African pedigree—and peanuts (also known as groundnuts) depend on being served with fresh, separate-grained rice. Hoppin' John had a sister dish in Limpin' Susan, which is stewed okra over rice. Sometimes, in okra season, peas and okra might be combined and served over hot rice. In Louisiana, rice complements shrimp Creole, every type of gumbo, crawfish étouffée, and grillades when grits are not desired or at hand. Rice became the signature dressing in Louisiana for stuffing birds, whereas in the Upper South it was prepared from cornbread. Rice calas or fritters, another West African carryover, were often sold piping hot and covered in powdered sugar in the streets of New Orleans, an alternative to beignets.

Commonly forgotten parts of the rice kitchen are rice breads, rice pancakes, and rice waffles, but these are being recognized again by cooks who appreciate rice's delicate flavor, as well as by those who must avoid wheat for health reasons. Championed in the 1847 classic cookbook *The Carolina Housewife* and popular in *Charleston Receipts*, a Junior League cookbook first published in 1950, and other community cookbooks, rice breads historically represented a fusion of African, European, and Native American cuisines. There were once *thousands* of recipes for rice bread, each one designed for the likes and needs of a particular household, but once wheat became cheaper thanks to the railroads in the early twentieth century, rice wasn't needed to economically replace a quarter of a loaf's volume, and rice bread fell out of fashion.

Rice as dessert was once important for the same reason—the cook could use rice leftovers and avoid using then-costlier wheat flour to make a pie or cake. Today, rice breads are making a comeback in Low Country cuisine, and they still are popular in Sierra Leone and Liberia, where some Africans returned after emancipation in the Americas in the nineteenth century.

As immigrants from around the world came to the South after the Civil War and through the post–civil rights era, new dishes arrived and helped to anchor southern rice cooking traditions. Chinese immigrants arriving in the Mississippi Delta and southern cities made stir-fries with collard greens and crawfish to go with their rice. Italians immigrating to the United States in increasing numbers after 1880 brought risottos and arancine. Sephardic Jews from Rhodes and Greece brought pink rice to Atlanta and Montgomery. Vietnamese arrivals in Houston and Louisiana innovated Viet-Cajun dishes, making delicious rice flour crepes and assembling traditional banh mi sandwiches on the airy rice-wheat bread they could make with a traditional blend. Cuban rice and beans has long since joined other rice pilaus in southern cooking, with the key difference being that moros y cristianos is not prepared in one pot.

Yes, rice has maintained its popularity because it is a part of so many culinary cultures, as we have seen here. There is, however, another important, and simple, reason for its popularity: rice works beautifully with a wide range of ingredients. It loves every liquid, from broth to coconut milk. Dried fruits and nuts pair wonderfully with it. Rice can become a salad with citrus, celery, and curry powder at hand. It seems almost married to tomatoes and magically attracts fish and shellfish. Give it almost any spice or herb, and it knows how to dance.

Historical but Not Stuck in the Past

Rice is a part of our history, but it has not remained in the past. The recipes in this book tell the story of how southerners of all backgrounds have expanded the repertoire of southern cuisine by introducing traditional rice dishes from around the globe or embracing rice dishes brought to the region by successive waves of migration. While southerners eagerly devour new approaches to one of their favorite ingredients, rice's devotees also appeal to tradition. Rice dishes are inspiration for fusion, innovation, and a return to classic recipes, and I am delighted to include *all* of these types of dishes in this book.

A potently personal (for me and many others) southern ingredient, rice is suitable in its traditional role as partner to legume and animal proteins as much as it happily accompanies gluten-free, vegan, and vegetarian dishes. A touch of innovation or return to tradition meld equally well with rice. The recipes included in this volume reflect, as rice must, its cultural diversity and historic journeys—but they just as much aim to give readers of various dietary stripes a reason to rush into the kitchen to cook and enjoy dishes familiar or new. I hope you enjoy this journey through my favorite, ever-flexible, expressive, and satisfying southern staple: rice.

The Basics

The rice kitchen requires the mastery of certain skills to guarantee the right textures and flavors. The seasonings, stocks, and cooking methods introduced in this section will be referenced in the rest of the cookbook to help you build layers of taste to elevate rice from mere background to center stage.

Kitchen Pepper

Kitchen pepper is an old-school spice mixture that was very popular in early American cooking, especially in the coastal South. While it takes its main cues from quatre épices, a spice mix of pepper, cloves, nutmeg, and ground ginger common in French cooking, it also helped to preserve both medieval and Silk Road flavors in southern foodways, as well as the flavors of West Africa, where indigenous and Middle Eastern spices had long influenced the cuisine. This is my take on this classic. It has the complexity of garam masala without quite the punch and heat.

MAKES ABOUT ½ CUP

- 2 tablespoons coarsely ground black pepper
- 1 tablespoon freshly grated nutmeg
- 1 tablespoon ground allspice
- 1 tablespoon ground cinnamon
- 1 tablespoon ground ginger
- 1 tablespoon ground mace
- 1 tablespoon ground white pepper
- 1 tablespoon red pepper flakes

Combine the ingredients in a small bowl. Store in an airtight container in a cool, dry place for up to six months.

Southern Dry Rice

This basic recipe results in rice with that separate-grain quality that coastal southerners have revered for generations, since the arrival of rice cookery from West Africa. Your pot, stove, and patience are very important factors, so experiment to see what combination works best for your cooking style. The finished rice should be al dente, not mushy!

MAKES 4 SERVINGS

1 cup long-grain white rice
1½ cups water or low-sodium chicken, beef, or vegetable
    stock, homemade (pages 18–22) or store-bought
2 tablespoons unsalted butter or 1 tablespoon extra-virgin
    olive oil (optional)
½ teaspoon kosher salt

Place the rice in a heavy-bottomed medium pot with a tight-fitting lid, cover with water, drain in a fine-mesh strainer, and return it to the pot. Do this three or four times, until the water runs clear. Cover the rice with water one last time and let it soak for about 5–10 minutes, then drain.

Add the remaining ingredients to the pot. Quickly bring the mixture to a boil over high heat. Stir once with a fork to make sure it isn't sticking, then cover with the lid. Turn the heat down to low and simmer very slowly until the liquid has been absorbed, about 15–20 minutes. Turn off the heat and let the rice sit for another 20–60 minutes for maximum absorption and steaming. Fluff lightly with a fork before serving.

Chicken Stock

This is my version of a classic chicken stock. It adds serious flavor to any rice dish, soup, or sauce. Enjoy the addition of a few whole cloves—my grandmother said this was a secret to a stock that would sing! Let the luscious chicken fat wink back at you.

MAKES ABOUT 1½ QUARTS

---

1 (4-pound) chicken carcass, cut into 4 pieces,
   including neck and back
8 whole cloves
4 celery stalks with the leaves, halved crosswise
4 medium carrots, peeled and halved crosswise
1 large yellow onion, quartered
1 medium parsnip, peeled and cut into 1-inch chunks
1 medium turnip, peeled and cut into 1-inch chunks
2 garlic cloves, peeled and smashed
5 sprigs fresh flat-leaf parsley with stems
5 sprigs fresh thyme
2 dried bay leaves
8–10 whole black peppercorns
7 cups cold water

Stud each of the 4 chicken pieces with 2 whole cloves. Place the chicken, vegetables, herbs, and peppercorns in a stockpot and add the 7 cups of water, or enough to cover the ingredients by 1 inch. Bring to a hearty boil over high heat, then turn the heat down to medium-low and simmer, uncovered, for 4–5 hours. Skim the scum from the stock with a spoon or fine-mesh strainer every 10–15 minutes for the first hour of cooking and later as needed. Add hot water as needed to keep the solids submerged.

Strain the stock through a sturdy mesh strainer into another large pot or bowl. Discard the solids. For the sake of food safety, place the pot in a sink full of ice water and allow to cool until the stock dips below 40°. Place it in the refrigerator overnight so you can remove solidified fat from the surface of the liquid the next day. Keep the stock in the refrigerator, covered, for 3–4 days or in an airtight container in the freezer for 3–4 months.

Brown Roasted Beef Stock

This is a great stock for red-meat dishes containing rice, and a good base for gravies and soups. If you are bold, add an anchovy or two to "beef up" the umami factor of the meat and tomatoes. If you're squeamish about an anchovy or two being too fishy but still want to add more flavor, add a tablespoon or two of Worcestershire sauce instead.

MAKES ABOUT 1½ QUARTS

4 pounds short ribs or oxtail or beef neck bones

3 tablespoons sunflower, vegetable, or other
   neutral-tasting oil

4 garlic cloves, with peel, smashed

2 celery stalks, cut into thirds

2 medium carrots, peeled and cut into 2-inch pieces

2 medium yellow onions, with peel, quartered

1 cup boiling-hot water or red wine

1 (14.5-ounce) can stewed tomatoes

6 sprigs fresh flat-leaf parsley

4 sprigs fresh thyme

2 dried bay leaves

8–10 whole black peppercorns

Preheat the oven to 400°. Arrange the beef in a single layer in a large roasting pan. Drizzle it with the oil on both sides. Place the beef in the oven and roast until it begins to brown, about 45 minutes, turning once and stirring often for even browning. Add the vegetables to the roasting pan and stir well. Return the pan to the oven and roast until the vegetables are browned and tender and the bones are deeply browned, about 40 minutes.

Transfer the bones and vegetables to a large stockpot, then spoon off the excess fat and throw it away. Add the hot water to the roasting pan and deglaze the pan, gently scraping up any roasted debris from the bottom with a wooden spoon. Pour the contents of the roasting pan into the pot. Add enough water to cover the bones and vegetables by a few inches. Place over high heat and bring it to just under a boil, then turn the heat down to low. Add the tomatoes, herbs, and peppercorns and simmer, uncovered, for 6 hours, adding more hot water as necessary to keep everything submerged.

Strain the stock through a sturdy mesh strainer into another large pot or bowl. Discard the solids. For the sake of food safety, place the pot in a sink full of ice water and allow to cool until the stock dips below 40°. Place it in the refrigerator overnight so you can remove the solidified fat from the surface of the liquid the next day. Keep the stock in the refrigerator, covered, for 3–4 days or in an airtight container in the freezer for 3–4 months.

Vegetable Stock

This is a great recipe to use in vegetarian or vegan dishes. It adds color, scent, nutrients, and overall flavor, so use it in place of plain water in soups, stews, and savory dishes whenever possible.

MAKES ABOUT 2 QUARTS

---

1 medium yellow onion

3 or 4 whole cloves

3 celery stalks, chopped

2 medium carrots, peeled and cut into $\frac{1}{2}$-inch-thick rounds

2 medium parsnips, peeled and cut into $\frac{1}{2}$-inch-thick rounds

1 medium turnip, peeled and cut into 1-inch cubes

1 small yellow- or orange-fleshed sweet potato, peeled and
cut into 1-inch cubes

3 garlic cloves, peeled and smashed

1 bunch fresh flat-leaf parsley, chopped

8 cups water

1 teaspoon kosher salt

Freshly ground black pepper or Kitchen Pepper (page 16),
to taste

Stud the onion with the cloves. Place all the vegetables in a medium-to-large stockpot. Add the 8 cups of water, or enough to cover the vegetables by about 1 inch, and add the salt. Bring to a boil over high heat, then turn the heat down to low and simmer, uncovered, for 3 hours. Be sure to add hot water as needed so that the vegetables stay submerged. Taste and add more salt and pepper as desired.

Strain the stock through a sturdy mesh strainer into another large pot or bowl. Discard the solids. For the sake of food safety, place the pot in a sink full of ice water and allow to cool until the stock dips below 40°. Keep in the refrigerator, covered, for 3–4 days or in an airtight container in the freezer for 3–4 months.

Pan Gravy

There is nothing like southern rice and gravy. You can add cara-melized onions to the gravy for an even more extraordinary ex-perience, as my mother once did. And if you want to make this simple sauce far more complex, add a dash of Kitchen Pepper (page 16), red pepper flakes, or ground cayenne pepper.

MAKES JUST UNDER 1½ CUPS

2 tablespoons bacon fat or other cooking fat
2 teaspoons all-purpose flour
1¼ cups beef or chicken stock, homemade (pages 18–20)
    or store-bought, or water
Kosher salt and freshly ground black pepper or Kitchen
    Pepper (page 16), to taste
¼ cup white or lighter red wine (optional)

Melt the fat in a skillet over medium heat and stir in the flour until smooth. Carefully allow the flour to brown until it reaches a dark blonde or chestnut color, but under no circumstances allow it to become scorched. Using a sturdy whisk, gradually stir in the stock. Cook, stirring and scraping to loosen any roasted bits of crust that might be stuck to the pan, until the mixture begins to thicken and comes to a light bubble.

Turn the heat down to low and simmer, continuing to stir. Taste the gravy and season it with salt and a few grindings of pepper. Add the wine (if using), then simmer for about 5 min-utes more, until smooth.

Deep Origins

The southern rice kitchen ultimately owes its existence to centuries of rice growing and cooking in Africa and Asia. In this chapter we do a deep dive into contemporary forms of the traditional Old World dishes that give southern rice its spice, savor, and millennia-old heritage. Umami and peppery flavors partner with rice here, as well as legumes like beans, cowpeas, and peanuts.

Basic Jollof Rice

This famous West African rice is named after the Wolof people of Senegal and Gambia, who themselves call it benachin. Maggi, a popular imported bouillon cube ubiquitous in West Africa, has become part of the flavor profile of everything there. If you have access to an international market, it will have Maggi cubes, and you can use them to make a Maggi broth to replace the stock here— just follow the instructions on the package. Be careful—it tends be salty, so go lightly at first to find your bearings.

MAKES 4 SERVINGS

- 2 tablespoons vegetable oil
- 1 large yellow onion, chopped
- 2 garlic cloves, peeled and smashed
- 2 tablespoons tomato paste
- 1½ cups long-grain white rice, washed and drained
- 1 habanero pepper, seeded and chopped
- ½ teaspoon freshly ground black pepper or Kitchen Pepper (page 16)
- ½ teaspoon seasoned salt or jollof rice seasoning
- 2½ cups vegetable or chicken stock, homemade (pages 18 and 22) or store-bought, or Maggi broth

Heat the oil in a medium saucepan with a tight-fitting lid over medium-high heat. Add the onion and garlic and sauté for 4–5 minutes, until soft. Add the tomato paste, turn the heat down to medium-low, and cook for about 3 minutes, stirring constantly. Stir in the rice, chili pepper, black pepper, and seasoned salt. Cook for 2–3 minutes, stirring constantly to prevent the rice from sticking to the bottom of the pan. Add the stock, cover, turn the heat down to low, and simmer for about 20 minutes, until the liquid is nearly but not completely absorbed.

Remove the lid, place a piece of aluminum foil over the pan, return the lid to the pan over the foil, and steam for another 20 minutes.

Wanda Blake's Jollof Rice

Chef Wanda Blake traces her origins to Louisiana and Arkansas. This is her version of the transnational West African classic jollof rice, which she created from recipes she encountered in her frequent travels in Nigeria. This is a great introduction to all of the key flavors of West Africa—smoky, funky, fruity, spicy, umami, earthy. You can add and subtract ingredients based on your comfort level.

MAKES 4–6 SERVINGS

---

1 pound Roma tomatoes, roughly chopped

1 red bell pepper, seeded and roughly chopped

½ medium yellow onion, roughly chopped

½ habanero pepper, seeded and roughly chopped

1 tablespoon kosher salt

1 cup water

2 tablespoons extra-virgin olive oil

2 cups long-grain white rice, washed and drained

1 tablespoon African or Jamaican curry powder

1 tablespoon shrimp powder (optional)

1 tablespoon smoked fish powder or smoked paprika (optional)

For the red sauce: Place the tomatoes, red bell pepper, onion, habanero pepper, salt, and water in a food processor and purée. Taste, and if you want it hotter, add some habanero seeds. The more you add, the hotter it will be.

For the rice: Place the olive oil in a medium pot over medium heat. Add the rice and sauté for 3–5 minutes. Add the red sauce, curry powder, shrimp powder (if using), and smoked fish powder (if using). Turn the heat up to high, bring to a boil, and boil for 5 minutes. Turn the heat down to low and cover. Cook until the rice is done, about 30–40 minutes.

Liberian Rice Bread

This is a standard recipe for Liberian rice bread with advice from my cousin, Chef Oliver Saye, who cooks from the perspective of his (our) Liberian heritage. We discovered through genetic genealogy that we are blood relatives from the era of the slave trade. Gullah-Geechee communities in South Carolina and Georgia and beyond have roots in Liberia and neighboring Sierra Leone.

MAKES 8 SERVINGS

2 cups ground rice

⅓ cup lightly packed light or dark brown sugar

1 tablespoon plus 1 teaspoon baking powder

1 teaspoon freshly grated nutmeg

1 teaspoon ground cinnamon

1 teaspoon ground ginger

½ teaspoon kosher salt

4-6 large overripe bananas, mashed (2 cups)

2 large eggs or egg substitute

1 cup whole milk or unsweetened coconut milk

½ cup canola oil

Preheat the oven to 325°. Grease one large or two small loaf pans.

Put all the dry ingredients in a large mixing bowl and stir until well combined. Put the bananas, eggs, milk, and oil in a separate large bowl and beat with a mixer or by hand until well combined. Add the wet ingredients to the dry ingredients and stir to mix thoroughly.

Pour the batter into the prepared loaf pan(s) and bake for 50–60 minutes, until a toothpick inserted in the center comes out clean.

Ghanaian Crab Stew

Eaten with rice or kenkey, a fermented corn dish, this dish from Ghana influenced later dishes like perloo and shrimp and grits. Sometimes okra is added, and there you have it: a grandfather dish to gumbo. For real Ghanaian flavor, provide additional hot peppers at the table and double up on the garlic and ginger for more punch. This is to be savored, not gulped!

MAKES 4–6 SERVINGS

- 1 medium yellow onion or 6 green onions, green and white parts, minced
- 1 habanero pepper, seeded and minced
- 2 tablespoons vegetable oil
- 2 medium tomatoes, peeled and chopped
- 1 green or red bell pepper, seeded and diced
- 1 pound cooked blue crab meat
- 2 teaspoons minced ginger or ginger paste
- 2 teaspoons minced garlic or garlic paste
- $\frac{1}{2}$ teaspoon Kitchen Pepper (page 16)
- $\frac{1}{2}$ teaspoon kosher salt
- $\frac{3}{4}$ cup vegetable, chicken, or beef stock, homemade (pages 18–22) or store-bought
- Chopped parsley, for garnish
- 4 cups cooked long-grain white rice, for serving

In a medium bowl, mix together the onion and habanero. Heat the oil in a large Dutch oven over medium-high heat, add the onion and peppers, and cook for 5–7 minutes, until soft. Add the tomatoes and bell pepper to the pan. Sauté, stirring frequently, until the tomatoes begin to soften and break down, about 10 minutes.

Flake the crab meat into the pan and add the ginger, garlic, kitchen pepper, salt, and stock. Stir, turn the heat down to low, and simmer, uncovered, for about 15 minutes, stirring occasionally. Garnish with chopped parsley and serve with rice.

Waakye

Traditional waakye is made with millet stalks, which turn the dish a deep wine-red. You can enhance the vegetable stock with water from a cup of soaked dried Jamaica flowers (also known as Jamaican sorrel or dried hibiscus flowers) to make the dish red. Red or not, this dish of cowpeas—which are called waakye (pronounced "wah-cheh") in Hausa, the lingua franca of West Africa—and rice (shinkafa da waakye means "rice and beans") is one of the clear ancestral dishes of Hoppin' John (page 91). It is hearty, sans meat, and very affordable, and this recipe is easy to double for a crowd.

MAKES 4–6 SERVINGS

---

1 cup dried black-eyed peas, sorted and soaked in
    water overnight
3 cups vegetable stock, homemade (page 22)
    or store-bought
1–2 tablespoons coconut oil
½ cup chopped yellow onion
2 garlic cloves, minced
1 cup long-grain white rice, washed and drained
2 dried bay leaves
½ teaspoon baking soda
½ teaspoon kosher salt

Drain the black-eyed peas and rinse well. Put them in a saucepan with a tight-fitting lid, add the stock, and place over high heat. Bring to a boil, then turn the heat down to low and simmer, uncovered, for 30–40 minutes.

After the black-eyed peas have been boiling for about 30 minutes, heat the oil in a skillet over medium-high heat. Add the onion and garlic and sauté until the onion is translucent, about 5 minutes, then add them to the black-eyed peas with the rice, bay leaves, baking soda, and salt.

Return the water to a boil, then turn the heat down to low and cook, covered, until the rice and beans are tender, about 30 minutes. Check the rice during cooking to make sure it doesn't scorch, and remove the lid, if necessary, to cook off any excess water when the rice and beans are tender.

Groundnut Stew My Way

Eating groundnut (peanut) stew and rice is one of my fondest memories from my first few trips to West Africa. This is yet another transnational dish that has earned its place in the canon of African food. It's so satisfying when you're hungry and want to hit all the notes, and it's certainly evocative of the southern peanut soups it can claim as its descendants.

MAKES 4–6 SERVINGS

2 pounds boneless, skinless chicken breasts or bone-in
   chicken thighs or legs

FOR THE MARINADE
1 large red onion, quartered
4 garlic cloves, peeled and smashed
1 (2-inch) knob of ginger, peeled and roughly chopped
1 very small habanero pepper, seeded and chopped
1 bouillon cube, ground to a powder, or 2 teaspoons
   bouillon granules
1 teaspoon coarsely ground black pepper
2 tablespoons tomato paste
2 tablespoons vegetable oil

2 tablespoons palm oil
2 cups vegetable or beef stock, homemade (pages 20–22)
   or store-bought
1 cup unsweetened smooth peanut butter
2 large tomatoes, chopped, or 1 (28-ounce) can diced
   tomatoes, drained
2 or 3 dried bay leaves
2 or 3 sprigs fresh thyme
4 cups cooked long-grain white rice, hot, for serving

Score and slash the chicken all over to really allow the seasonings to take hold, then place it in a baking dish. Put all of the marinade ingredients in a food processor and process until liquefied. Pour the marinade over the chicken, cover, and place in the refrigerator to marinate for several hours or overnight. When you're ready to cook, cut the marinated chicken breasts into smaller bite-size pieces.

In a large Dutch oven over medium heat, melt the palm oil. Add the chicken pieces and sauté for about 20 minutes. Add a little liquid if it starts to brown too much.

Add the stock, peanut butter, and tomatoes and stir well. Add the bay leaves and thyme. Turn the heat down to low and simmer, uncovered, for 45 minutes, stirring for about 3 minutes every 15 minutes. After 45 minutes, the liquid should be reduced by more than one-third.

Remove the bay leaves and thyme sprigs before serving, and serve with hot white rice.

NOTE ❈ Adding an earthy and marine flavor element, such as smoked fish powder, to this stew can give it a nice background umami. But I don't like smoked fish, so I suggest the following seasonings instead: 2 teaspoons bonito flakes, seaweed flakes, ground crayfish, or shrimp powder, or 1 tablespoon oyster or oyster mushroom sauce. If you choose to add any of these to your pot, add it with the bay leaves and thyme and give the stew another 10 minutes.

Thiebou Niebe

Pronounced "cheb oo nyay-bay," this is a classic Senegalese dish of black-eyed peas and rice. My recipe here is an adaptation of my friend Chef Pierre Thiam's masterly version. It stars jewellike veggies studding fragrant, deeply flavored rice. It's ideal for parties, holidays, or big group dinners.

MAKES 6–8 SERVINGS

¼ cup peanut oil

3 plum tomatoes, chopped

1 medium yellow onion, minced

¼ cup plus 1 tablespoon tomato paste

1 tablespoon chopped fresh parsley

1 tablespoon chopped garlic

1 teaspoon kosher salt

2 quarts vegetable stock, homemade (page 22)
 or store-bought

¾ cup dried black-eyed peas (¼ pound), sorted and
 soaked for at least 1 hour

6 medium carrots, peeled and halved crosswise

1 medium head of cabbage, quartered

½ pound yuca, peeled and cut into large chunks, or
 yellow- or white-fleshed sweet potatoes

3–4 tablespoons Vietnamese fish sauce (optional)

2 medium eggplants, quartered

1 medium butternut squash (about 2 pounds), peeled,
 quartered, and seeded

6 okra pods, trimmed

2 habanero peppers, seeded and chopped

3 recipes Southern Dry Rice (page 17), using basmati rice

Heat the oil in a large pot with a tight-fitting lid over medium-low heat. Add the tomatoes, onion, and tomato paste and stir well. Add the parsley, garlic, and salt and stir to combine. Cover and simmer for about 15 minutes, then pour in the stock, cover again, and bring to a boil over high heat.

Drain the black-eyed peas and add them to the pot along with the carrots, cabbage, yuca, and fish sauce. Turn the heat down to low and simmer, uncovered, for about 30 minutes. Add the eggplants, butternut squash, okra, and habaneros, and simmer, uncovered, until tender, about 10 minutes. Taste and adjust the seasonings as desired.

Place the rice on a serving dish. With a slotted spoon, transfer the vegetables and black-eyed peas to the dish and then pour 2 ladlefuls of jus over them.

Omo Tuo (Rice Balls)

When I went to West Africa, I didn't really like fufu, mashed and pounded yam with a gluey texture, but I loved rice balls, which are another starchy instrument for dipping and eating traditional stews. They are less gluey and lighter than fufu and are more easily digested. Serve them with Groundnut Stew My Way (page 34) or Sweet Potato Leaf Stew (page 39), if you please!

MAKES 2–4 RICE BALLS

3 cups water

1 cup short-grain white rice

1 teaspoon kosher salt

Put all the ingredients in a large saucepan with a tight-fitting lid and bring to a boil over high heat. Cover and turn the heat down to low. Let the rice cook for 20 minutes, then uncover and continue simmering until any extra water has gently cooked off, then remove the pan from the heat. Stir occasionally to prevent sticking and sprinkle in a little more water if needed. When the rice is soft, mash it with a wooden spoon or potato masher. It doesn't need to be smooth; the most important thing is the rice is sticking together.

Let the rice cool further until you can handle it, then, using a large, wet mixing spoon, take up a spoonful of mashed rice. With wet hands, shape the rice quickly into a firm, smooth ball the size of a tennis ball and set aside. Repeat with the remaining rice. You should get 2–4 rice balls.

Sweet Potato Leaf Stew

This is the original greens with rice. This version is from the Rice Coast of West Africa. The flavor profile of sweet potato leaves is akin to spinach meeting collard greens. If you cannot find sweet potato leaves in a market and don't grow them yourself, substitute finely shredded collards and spinach mixed together.

MAKES 2–4 SERVINGS

- 2 pounds sweet potato leaves, washed and stemmed
- ¼ teaspoon kosher salt
- ½ cup peanut or vegetable oil
- 2 medium tomatoes, finely chopped
- 1 small yellow onion, finely chopped
- 1 green bell pepper, seeded and diced
- 1 garlic clove, finely chopped
- 1 cup finely chopped unsalted roasted peanuts (optional)
- ¼ teaspoon ground cayenne pepper, or to taste
- 1 cup vegetable stock, homemade (page 22) or store-bought
- 4 cups cooked long-grain white rice, hot, for serving

Tear the sweet potato leaves into small pieces or cut them into very thin strips. Fill a small saucepan with water, add the salt, and place the pan over high heat. When the water is boiling, drop in the pieces of sweet potato leaves. Cook quickly, uncovered, until the leaves are soft, about 10–15 minutes. Drain the leaves and purée them briefly in a blender until semismooth. Set aside.

Heat the oil in a skillet over medium-high heat. Add the tomatoes, onion, bell pepper, and garlic, and cook, stirring frequently, for several minutes, until the onion is soft. Add the peanuts (if using) and ground cayenne pepper and cook for 5–10 minutes. Add the sweet potato leaves, stir, and cook for 2 minutes. Add the stock and gently cook, uncovered, for 15 minutes, or until the liquid is reduced by at least half. Serve with hot white rice.

Taste Transitions

Rice was brought to the American mainland and then became a part of Island and coastal cookery as trade moved staples and ingredients between the ports of the Chesapeake Bay, the Carolinas, and the Gulf Coast. Here we meet the cousin dishes of the southern rice table—spicy, savory, complex dishes with Afri-Creole taste notes that bridge the Old World and New.

Haitian Red Beans and Rice

Before there was Louisiana, there was Saint-Domingue. In this French colony in the Caribbean, African, Native, and Western European flavors collided to create a New World Creole cuisine. This red-beans-and-rice dish is spicier, creamier, and more cosmopolitan than your typical version and should be eaten with Haitian Pikliz (page 44) handy!

MAKES 4 SERVINGS

1 cup dried kidney beans

1½ teaspoons kosher salt, divided

Freshly ground black pepper, to taste

6 cups water

2–3 cups vegetable or chicken stock, homemade (pages 18 and 22) or store-bought

3 tablespoons lard or extra-virgin olive oil

1 medium yellow onion, minced

2 garlic cloves, minced

2 teaspoons ground ginger or minced fresh ginger

1 cup unsweetened coconut milk

1 Scotch bonnet pepper, seeded and minced (optional)

½ teaspoon ground cloves

2 sprigs fresh thyme

3 cups long-grain white rice, washed and drained

Place the beans in a large fine-mesh strainer or colander and rinse under running water until the draining water runs clear. Transfer them to a medium Dutch oven and add ½ teaspoon of the salt and a few grindings of pepper. Pour in the water, place over high heat, and bring to a boil. Turn the heat down to low and simmer, partially uncovered, for about 1½ hours, or until the beans are tender. Drain the beans in a fine-mesh strainer set over a deep bowl and set aside. Retain the water the beans were cooked in and add enough chicken or vegetable stock to make 1 quart. Keep the beans moist and warm for the time being by placing them in a bowl and covering it with a tea towel or lid.

Wash and dry the Dutch oven, then return it to the stovetop over medium-high heat. Place the lard in the pot, and when it's hot but not smoking, add the onion, garlic, and ginger. Cook until the onion is translucent, about 5 minutes.

Stir in the 1 quart of reserved bean broth, the coconut milk, Scotch bonnet, cloves, thyme, the remaining teaspoon of salt, and a liberal grinding of pepper. Add the rice and stir to combine. Cover the pot with a tight-fitting lid and turn the heat down to low. Simmer undisturbed for about 25 minutes, or until the rice is tender and has absorbed all the liquid.

Remove the pot from the heat and stir in the beans. Let the dish sit, covered, for 15–20 minutes to allow the flavors to blend, then serve immediately.

Haitian Pikliz

This is the must-have condiment for all Haitian dishes. A Haitian answer to chow-chow, it adds color and flavor to just about any Island dish, and you can make it as spicy or mild as you like. Some pikliz are sneaky and pack a slap when you least expect it.

MAKES 2–3 CUPS

1 large carrot, peeled
2 cups shredded cabbage
2 green onions, both green and white parts, thinly sliced
1 medium yellow onion, thinly sliced
1 cup thinly sliced mixed bell peppers (green, orange, red)
2 whole Scotch bonnet peppers
Juice of 1 lime
2 teaspoons turbinado sugar
1 teaspoon kosher salt
12–14 whole black peppercorns
4 garlic cloves, peeled and smashed
4 whole cloves
2 or 3 whole allspice berries
2 cups white, cane, or apple cider vinegar

Using a vegetable peeler, slice the carrot into shavings. Combine the carrot shavings, cabbage, green onions, onion, and bell peppers in a large mixing bowl. Add the Scotch bonnet peppers and the lime juice, then mix in the sugar, salt, peppercorns, garlic, cloves, and allspice berries and stir well.

Pack the mixture into a 1-quart Mason jar, then pour in the vinegar until the jar is full. Screw on the jar lid and place the jar in the refrigerator to marinate for about 5 days before using. After opening, keep in the refrigerator for up to 4–6 weeks.

Coconut Rice

This creamy rice from Africa and the Caribbean is a nice alternative to plain rice. If you like hot, buttery rice, this will feel good to your soul. I feel as if this dish was probably enjoyed a few times in the Low Country, where coconuts invariably figured into the cuisine.

MAKES 6–8 SERVINGS

---

3 cups long-grain white rice, such as basmati or jasmine,
   washed and drained
$3\frac{1}{2}$–4 cups water
$1\frac{1}{2}$ cups unsweetened full-fat coconut milk
1 teaspoon kosher salt
Freshly ground black pepper, to taste

Combine all of the ingredients in a large pot with a tight-fitting lid over high heat and bring to a boil. Boil for about 5 minutes, then turn the heat down to low and cover. Simmer for about 25 minutes, then remove the pot from the heat and allow the rice to continue to steam, still covered. Check after about 15 minutes and add a little water if the rice becomes too dry before the grains are tender. Fluff with a fork before serving.

Shawanda Marie's
Laundry Day Red Beans and Rice

Shawanda is a native of Louisiana, an expert on Afri-Creole culture, and a native speaker of Louisiana Creole. This is a recipe she shared with me for the Louisiana classic red beans and rice, for laundry day. This is a pork-free dish, but you can add a cup or two of andouille sausage in the third step to stew along with the beans as they get creamy, if that's your fancy.

MAKES 4–6 SERVINGS

2 cups dried red kidney beans (Camellia brand if possible)

3 cups chicken stock, homemade (page 18) or store-bought, plus more if needed

2 tablespoons vegetable oil

1 large yellow onion, chopped

1 green bell pepper, seeded and chopped

4 celery stalks, chopped

2 teaspoons garlic powder, or more to taste

1 teaspoon ground cayenne pepper, or more to taste

$\frac{1}{2}$ to 1 teaspoon ground dried thyme

1 or 2 dried bay leaves

Kosher salt and freshly ground black pepper, to taste

2 teaspoons minced garlic, or more to taste

4–6 cups cooked long-grain white rice, hot, for serving

You may soak the beans overnight, if desired. If you do, when you're ready to cook, drain the water. Place the beans in a large pot with a tight-fitting lid, then add the stock so it reaches twice as high up the sides of the pot as the beans. Bring to a rolling boil over high heat. Boil the beans, uncovered, for about 1 hour, until they're tender but not falling apart. Check the beans occasionally and add water or stock as needed to ensure they're always covered by liquid; otherwise they will become discolored and hard.

When the beans have about 10 minutes more to cook, place the vegetable oil in a skillet over medium-high heat. Add the onion, bell pepper, celery, and seasonings and sauté until the onion turns translucent, about 5 minutes. Add the garlic and sauté for 2 minutes more, stirring occasionally. Remove from the heat.

Drain the beans through a large strainer and return them to the pot. Add the sautéed vegetables and just enough stock or water to cover the beans and vegetables. Bring to a boil, then turn the heat down to low. Cover and simmer for at least 2 hours, preferably 3, until everything gets soft and creamy. Stir occasionally to make sure that nothing burns or sticks to the bottom of the pot. Taste and adjust the seasonings as you go along.

To serve, ladle the beans over hot long-grain rice.

Diverse Approaches

The South is more than its past and stereotypical dishes. It's also a thriving region where global ingredients like coconut oil, garam masala, and cinnamon leaf now sit beside the salsa, sriracha, and coriander that help make rice the virtuoso of the kitchen.

Nancie McDermott's Thai-Style Chicken Hidden in Curried Rice

My good friend Chef Nancie McDermott, author of the Savor the South *book* Fruit, *spent a formative period in Thailand during her years in the Peace Corps. She graciously shared with me her crowd-pleasing recipe for Thai chicken and curry rice, which I think is stunning. Served with any Thai soup, fresh spring rolls, fresh tropical fruit for dessert, and a refreshing Thai iced tea, this becomes the center of a sparkling dinner from a world-class cuisine.*

MAKES 6–8 SERVINGS

3 tablespoons vegetable oil

$3/4$ cup coarsely chopped yellow onion

1 tablespoon peeled and roughly chopped garlic

5 quarter-sized slices fresh ginger (optional)

1 tablespoon curry powder (see Note)

$1^{1}/_{2}$ teaspoons kosher salt

$1/2$ teaspoon freshly ground black pepper

4–6 bone-in, skin-on chicken thighs or legs, or a combination ($1^{1}/_{2}$–2 pounds)

2 cups long-grain white rice, washed and drained

$3^{1}/_{2}$ cups chicken stock or water

3 green onions, finely chopped

$1/3$ cup coarsely chopped fresh cilantro

FOR GARNISH (OPTIONAL)

$1/2$ cup thinly sliced shallots, fried in vegetable oil until golden brown and crisp

Cucumber slices

Set a medium bowl and tongs by the stove to hold the chicken after browning. In a large, deep pot with a tight-fitting lid, such as a Dutch oven, heat the oil over medium-high heat. When a bit of onion added to the oil sizzles at once, the oil is ready. Add the garlic, onion, and ginger (if using). Toss well and cook just until shiny and fragrant, about 1 minute. Add the curry powder, salt, and pepper, and cook, tossing often, until the onion and garlic have softened but not browned, 1–2 minutes. Add the chicken pieces, skin-side down, and let them cook for 2–3 minutes, turning once or twice, until they are well-coated with spices and beginning to brown. Use the tongs to transfer the partially cooked chicken to the bowl and set it aside.

Add the rice to the pot and cook, tossing often, until it's evenly colored with spices and turning white. Add the chicken stock and stir well. Increase the heat to high and bring to a lively boil. Stir well and cook for 1 minute, then adjust the heat to maintain a visible but gentle boil and cook, stirring now and then, until the rice swells and absorbs most of the liquid, 10–15 minutes.

Turn the heat down to medium-low and return the chicken pieces to the pot, along with any juices in the bowl. Tuck the chicken pieces into the partially cooked rice so they're touching the bottom of the pot, smooth the rice over the chicken pieces to cover them, and then cover the pot. Cook, undisturbed, until the rice is tender and the chicken is cooked through (the internal temperature should reach 165°), 45–55 minutes. When both the chicken and the rice are done, remove the pot from the heat and let it stand, covered, for at least 10 minutes (longer is fine).

Transfer the chicken to a platter and gently fluff the rice with a fork. Add most of the green onions and cilantro to the rice, reserving a little of each for garnish, and toss to mix them into the rice evenly.

To serve, return the chicken to the pot and garnish with the reserved cilantro and green onions. Or transfer the rice to a serving platter, mounding it up handsomely, place the chicken around the edges of the rice, and garnish with the reserved green onions and cilantro. Either way, garnish with the fried shallots and cucumber slices (if using). Serve hot or warm.

To serve the dish for a crowd, place the cooked chicken pieces on a cutting board, carefully pull the meat and skin from the bones, and chop coarsely. Return the meat to the pot and stir to mix it in with the rice, then serve the chicken-rice mixture directly from the pot or mounded on a platter as above, garnished with the green onions, cilantro, and shallots and cucumber slices (if using).

NOTE ✽ Use this simple spice mixture in place of curry powder if you have time to gather and stir a few aromatic ground spices together: 1 teaspoon ground cumin; 1 teaspoon ground coriander; 1 teaspoon ground turmeric; ½ teaspoon ground cinnamon; ½ teaspoon ground cayenne pepper (or more for more heat).

Curried Rice Salad

This is a very summery southern rice dish that makes a great side dish at a barbecue or family reunion. It can also serve as a stand-alone entrée for a vegetarian or vegan meal.

MAKES 4–6 SERVINGS

FOR THE DRESSING

2 tablespoons white wine vinegar

1 garlic clove, peeled and smashed

2 rounded teaspoons curry powder

1 teaspoon sugar

Pinch of seasoned salt

$\frac{1}{2}$ teaspoon freshly ground black pepper

$\frac{1}{4}$ cup extra-virgin olive oil

3 cups cooked long-grain white rice, at room temperature

$\frac{3}{4}$ cup thinly sliced green onion

$\frac{1}{2}$ cup currants or roughly chopped raisins (optional)

$\frac{1}{2}$ cup diced celery

In a medium bowl, whisk together the vinegar, garlic, curry powder, sugar, seasoned salt, and pepper. Slowly whisk in the oil. Let the mixture stand for 15–30 minutes, then taste and adjust the seasonings as desired. Remove and discard the garlic clove.

In a large bowl, gently toss together the rice, green onion, currants (if using), and celery. Fold in the dressing until it's evenly mixed. Cover and place in the refrigerator until chilled, at least 1 hour. Just before serving, taste, adjust the seasonings if desired, and gently toss to mix. Serve cool.

African American Soul Fried Rice

This is my take on a southern stir-fried rice dish, using common southern and soul food ingredients. Traditionally, many soul and Creole dishes were built around leftover rice; these predated dishes built around leftover takeout fried rice from Chinese restaurants, which have made their impact on southern Black communities. This recipe blends it all up to see what happens. The fresher the vegetable stars in the dish, the better.

Soumbala, or netetou, is African locust bean paste. It is commonly available at West African or international markets. If you can't find it, you can substitute your favorite low-sodium soy sauce.

MAKES 4–6 SERVINGS

- 2 tablespoons canola or peanut oil, divided
- 4 green onions, green and white parts, thinly sliced on the bias
- 2 garlic cloves, thinly sliced
- 1 tablespoon minced fresh ginger
- 1½ teaspoons kosher salt
- 1 teaspoon red pepper flakes, ground cayenne pepper, or hot sauce, or more to taste
- 1 cup diced red, yellow, and green bell peppers
- 1 cup thinly sliced (think ribbons!) collard greens
- ½ cup fresh okra, thinly sliced
- 4 cups cooked long-grain white rice
- 1 cup cooked black-eyed peas (see Note)
- 1 teaspoon soumbala or low-sodium soy sauce
- 1 cup scrambled eggs, cooked shrimp, leftover shredded poultry or meat, or tofu (optional)

Heat 1 tablespoon of the oil in a wok or large skillet over medium-high heat until very hot. Add the green onions, garlic, and ginger. Cook, stirring constantly, until they soften and release their scent, about 3 minutes. Add the remaining tablespoon of oil, the salt, and the red pepper flakes. Add the bell pepper, collard greens, and okra and sauté for another 3 minutes.

Add the rice, black-eyed peas, and soumbala, and cook, stirring frequently, until heated through, about 5 minutes. If using scrambled eggs, cooked shrimp, or leftover meat or tofu, add them at this point and cook until heated through, another 3 minutes.

NOTE ❋ The black-eyed peas should be just cooked until done and tender—not mushy!

Moros y Cristianos

This Cuban rice-and-beans dish is a staple of Miami's Calle Ocho and beyond. The name literally recalls the Reconquista, when Christian armies in the Middle Ages recaptured much of the Iberian Peninsula from African Muslims ("Moros," or "Moors," in the name), but it also doubles for the two main influences in Cuban civilization, other than Indigenous cultures: those of enslaved Africans and of European slaveholders and settlers. This dish is earthy, rich, tummy-filling goodness that requires a few good cups of Cuban coffee and light music afterward.

MAKES 5–6 SERVINGS

FOR THE BEANS

1 cup dried black beans
1 ham hock or smoked turkey neck
1/2 medium yellow onion, finely chopped
1/4 green bell pepper, seeded and finely chopped
1 teaspoon finely chopped garlic
9–10 cups vegetable stock, homemade (page 22)
  or store-bought

FOR THE RICE

4 bacon slices, cut into 1-inch pieces
2 tablespoons extra-virgin olive oil
1/2 medium yellow onion, finely chopped
1/4 green bell pepper, seeded and finely chopped
1 teaspoon finely chopped garlic
1 teaspoon dried oregano
1 teaspoon ground cumin
1 1/2 teaspoons kosher salt
1 teaspoon freshly ground black pepper

2 cups long-grain white rice, washed and drained
(converted rice works well)
Reserved cooking liquid (from above)

For the beans: Place the beans in a large fine-mesh strainer or colander and rinse under cold running water until the draining water runs clear. Transfer them to a large pot or Dutch oven and add the ham hock, onion, bell pepper, and garlic. Pour in the stock and bring to a boil over high heat. Turn the heat down to low and simmer, partially covered, for 2½–3 hours, until the beans are tender but still intact. Check on the beans occasionally and if the liquid seems to be evaporating too quickly, add more boiling water. When the beans are done, almost all of the cooking liquid should have cooked away. Pour the cooked beans and veggies into a fine-mesh strainer or colander set over a large bowl to catch the remaining cooking liquid, which will be used later to cook the rice. Reserve the cooking liquid to use later. Set the beans and veggies aside. Discard the ham hock.

For the rice: Pour the olive oil into a large pot with a tight-fitting lid over medium-high heat. Add the bacon and fry until crisp and brown. Remove the bacon from the pot with a slotted spoon and set it on paper towels to drain, leaving the fat in the pot. Add the onion, bell pepper, garlic, oregano, cumin, salt, and pepper to the pot. Cook, stirring frequently, for about 5 minutes, until the vegetables are soft but not brown—you do not want the sofrito to burn or brown.

Add the rice and heat it for a minute or two. Add the beans with veggies and the reserved cooking liquid, then add enough water to cover the rice by 1 inch. Turn the heat down to low and simmer, covered, for 25 minutes. Remove the pot from the heat and allow the beans and rice to rest for 15 minutes before serving.

Meyer Lemon Rice
with Candied Garlic

This is a good lemony rice that pairs well with chicken, fish, or chickpeas. The flavor of Meyer lemons is bright rather than overwhelming, and if you can find some, use them. But the sharper flavor of regular lemons work well, too, though you may need to experiment with the amount of juice used.

MAKES 3–4 SERVINGS

FOR THE RICE

- 2 cups fish stock or chicken or vegetable stock, homemade (pages 18 and 22) or store-bought
- 2 tablespoons Meyer lemon juice
- $1/2$ teaspoon kosher salt
- 1 sprig lemon thyme or lemon basil
- $1\frac{1}{4}$ cups long-grain or extra-long-grain white rice, washed and drained
- 1 tablespoon finely grated lemon zest
- 2 tablespoons unsalted butter or olive oil
- 1 tablespoon chopped fresh flat-leaf parsley
- Freshly ground black pepper, to taste

FOR THE CANDIED GARLIC

- $3/4$ cups vegetable, chicken, or beef stock, homemade (pages 18 and 22) or store-bought, or water
- 2 tablespoons sugar
- $1/4$ teaspoon kosher salt
- 8 garlic cloves, peeled and smashed
- 2 tablespoons extra-virgin olive oil

For the rice: Place the stock, lemon juice, salt, and herb sprig in a large, heavy-bottomed saucepan with a tight-fitting lid over high heat. Bring to a boil, then add the rice, cover, and turn the heat down to low. Simmer until the liquid is absorbed, about 20–25 minutes. Remove the pan from the heat. Stir in the lemon zest and let the pan stand, covered, for another 10 minutes. Stir in the butter and parsley and season to taste with pepper.

While the rice cooks, make the candied garlic: In a small saucepan, combine the stock, sugar, and salt and stir until the sugar is dissolved. Place the saucepan over medium heat and add the garlic. Cook the garlic for 20 minutes, or until soft. Place the olive oil in a skillet over medium-high heat. Using a slotted spoon, transfer the candied garlic to the skillet and lightly sauté for 5 minutes, until it turns a light golden-brown.

Dot the rice with the candied garlic before serving.

Sephardic Pink Rice

This is the traditional rice side dish of the Sephardic immigrants who came from Rhodes and other parts of the former Ottoman Empire and settled in Montgomery, Alabama, and Atlanta, Georgia. It dances well with everything from Mediterranean veggies and grilled salmon to Greek meatballs and marinated chicken seasoned with oregano or basil.

MAKES 4 SERVINGS

2 tablespoons vegetable oil

1 tablespoon extra-virgin olive oil

1 cup long-grain white rice, washed and drained

1 small yellow onion, diced

2 cups vegetable or chicken stock, homemade (pages 18 and 22) or store-bought

1/4 cup tomato sauce, or more to taste

1 teaspoon kosher salt

1/2 teaspoon freshly ground black pepper or Kitchen Pepper (page 16)

Place the oils, rice, and onion in a medium pot over medium-high heat. Stir to coat the rice with oil and cook for about 3 minutes, stirring often, until the rice and onion are translucent.

Place the broth, tomato sauce, salt, and pepper in a medium saucepan with a tight-fitting lid over high heat. Bring to a boil, add the rice and onion, stir, and bring to a boil again. Cover, turn the heat down to low, and simmer for 20 minutes. Check the mixture periodically and add water if the rice starts sticking to the pan. After 20 minutes, turn off the heat, stir the rice with a fork, and replace the lid. Let it stand, covered, on the burner for a few minutes. Serve warm.

Edna Lewis's Wild Rice

Even though wild rice (Zizania aquatica) grows throughout the Upper South, it was not traditionally used as in midwestern cooking. The legendary chef Edna Lewis of Freetown, Virginia, remembered that her mother let the family poultry get fattened up on wild rice. Here is an adaptation of her recipe featuring the grain.

MAKES 4 SERVINGS

1 cup wild rice, washed and drained
Pinch of chopped fresh thyme leaves
1½ cups cold water or chicken or vegetable stock, homemade (pages 18 and 22) or store-bought
1 tablespoon fat reserved from cooking a chicken, pheasant, or turkey, or unsalted butter
½ teaspoon kosher salt
¼ teaspoon freshly ground black pepper or Kitchen Pepper (page 16)

Put the rice in an enamel-covered Dutch oven and fill the pot with cold water. Crush the thyme leaves between your fingers and add them to the pot.

Set the pot over medium-high heat, add the cold water, and bring to a quick boil, then turn the heat down to low. Simmer, covered, for 1 hour, then stir in the salt, pepper, and fat. Continue cooking for 30 minutes more. If the rice seems too dry after 30 minutes, add ¼ cup water and continue to cook until all of the liquid is absorbed. Fluff it with a fork and serve.

Pati Jinich's Unforgettable Rice

My friend and Mexican chef extraordinaire Pati Jinich, host of the TV series Pati's Mexican Table, *generously shared this recipe for her version of a Mexican rice dish. This is another red rice dish in the Atlantic world contributed by enslaved Africans, in this case four centuries of Afro-Mexican heritage. The colors and flavors are comfy and visually delightful.*

MAKES 6–8 SERVINGS

- 2 cups long-grain or extra-long-grain white rice, washed and drained
- 2 tomatoes, quartered
- ⅓ cup roughly chopped white onion
- 2 garlic cloves, peeled
- 1½ teaspoons kosher salt
- 3 tablespoons safflower or corn oil
- 3½ cups chicken or vegetable stock, homemade (pages 18 and 22) or store-bought, or water
- 1 tablespoon fresh lime juice (optional)
- 2 sprigs parsley
- ¾ cup diced carrots (optional)
- ½ cup shelled green peas, fresh or frozen (optional)
- 1 or 2 serrano peppers (optional)

In a bowl, soak the rice in hot water for about 5 minutes, then drain it through a fine-mesh strainer and rinse with cold water.

While the rice soaks, purée the tomatoes in a blender along with the onion, garlic, and salt. Pour the mixture through a fine-mesh strainer into a bowl and set aside.

Heat the oil in a large saucepan with a tight-fitting lid (preferably transparent) over medium-high heat until hot but not smoking. Add the rice and sauté, stirring often, until the color of the rice changes to a milky white, 3–4 minutes.

Pour in the strained tomato purée, mix it gently, and let it cook until the purée has darkened and thickened and is mostly absorbed, about 3 minutes more. Stir in the stock and lime juice (if using), then give it a gentle stir and add the parsley and carrots, peas, and peppers (if using). Turn the heat up to high and let it all come to a boil, then cover, turn the heat down to low, and cook for about 20 minutes. The rice is ready when it's tender and most of the liquid has been absorbed but there is a lot of moisture in the pot. If the rice is not yet tender but the liquid has dried up, add a couple of tablespoons of water, replace the lid, and let it cook for a couple more minutes.

Remove the pan from the heat and let the rice sit, still covered, for at least 5 minutes, then fluff it with a fork and serve.

Autumn Herb Rice

Fall begs for a seasonally appropriate rice dish. This roast chicken–, root vegetable–, and pot roast–loving herb-flavored rice is a little touch of Texas meeting a harvest-season chicken dressing. You can easily make this meatless by using vegetable stock.

MAKES 4–6 SERVINGS

1/4 cup unsalted butter or margarine

3 tablespoons minced shallots

1 teaspoon minced garlic

2 cups converted rice, washed and drained

1 teaspoon paprika

1/2 teaspoon crushed dried rosemary

1/2 teaspoon ground dried sage

1/2 teaspoon ground dried marjoram

1/2 teaspoon ground dried thyme

1/2 teaspoon finely chopped fresh or ground dried basil

1 quart chicken or vegetable stock, homemade (pages 18 and 22) or store-bought, hot

2 fresh bay leaves

1/2 teaspoon seasoned salt

1/4 teaspoon freshly ground black pepper or Kitchen Pepper (page 16)

Place the butter, shallots, and garlic in a large sauté pan with a tight-fitting lid over medium-high heat and sauté for 5 minutes, until the shallots are translucent. Turn the heat down to low, add the rice, and cook for 10 minutes, until the rice is no longer opaque. Add the paprika and dried herbs, and then add the chicken stock. Add the bay leaves and stir well. Stir in the seasoned salt and pepper.

Turn the heat to high and bring to a boil. Boil for 5 minutes, then turn the heat down to low, cover, and simmer for 25 minutes, or until the rice is soft. Remove the pan from the heat and allow the rice to steam, still covered, for 10 minutes. Remove the bay leaves before serving.

Southern Classics

Rice stars on the southern table as in no other regional American cuisine. Even when it seems plebeian and plain, rice is just about irreplaceable when it comes to the amazingly versatile gravies, sauces, and soups it stars in.

Wanda Blake's Jambalaya

Chef Wanda Blake returns to her Louisiana roots with this hearty and true Louisiana jambalaya, an Afri-Creole pilau by any name that's related to jollof rice and red rice. The chili powder and smoked paprika take the place of the smoked fish powder used in West Africa.

MAKES 6–8 SERVINGS

1 pound Roma tomatoes

Kosher salt

½ cup dry sherry

½ cup Worcestershire sauce

2 tablespoons tomato paste

1 teaspoon lemon juice

1 teaspoon hot sauce

1 tablespoon chili powder

1 tablespoon smoked paprika

2 cups water

2 tablespoons extra-virgin olive oil

1 pound boneless chicken thighs, cut into bite-size pieces

1 red bell pepper, diced

2 celery stalks, diced

½ medium yellow onion, diced

4 garlic cloves, diced

4 cups long-grain white rice, washed and drained

½ pound medium prawns, peeled and deveined

Ground white pepper, to taste

Purée the tomatoes in a food processor, then sprinkle them with salt. In a medium bowl, combine the sherry, Worcestershire sauce, tomato paste, lemon juice, hot sauce, chili powder, and smoked paprika. Add the water, stir, and set aside.

Heat the olive oil in a saucepan with a tight-fitting lid over medium-high heat. Add the chicken, bell pepper, onion, garlic, and celery and sauté for 5 minutes, until chicken is halfway cooked. Add the tomatoes and seasoning mixture, turn the heat to high, and bring to a boil. Boil for 10 minutes, then taste the seasonings and adjust them as needed.

Add the rice and prawns and bring back to a boil, then turn the heat down to low and cover. Cook until the rice is tender, about 30–40 minutes. The jambalaya is finished when all the liquid is absorbed. Just before serving, add the white pepper and stir.

Okra Soup

This is one of my favorite recipes for revisiting the historical roots of southern cooking and its African heritage. Okra soup used to be a ubiquitous southern dish from the Chesapeake to the Low Country to the Lower Mississippi River valley and beyond. It is properly served over fresh-cooked rice to give it body and a place for all of the fresh flavors to land. This is a summer-centered dish, meant for the season.

MAKES 6–8 SERVINGS

1/4 cup unsalted butter

1 tablespoon lard or extra-virgin olive oil (use extra-virgin olive oil to keep kosher)

1 small yellow onion, diced and dusted with flour

2 tablespoons finely chopped fresh flat-leaf parsley

1 garlic clove, minced

1 sprig fresh thyme

1 teaspoon kosher salt

1/2 teaspoon Kitchen Pepper (page 16)

1/2 teaspoon red pepper flakes

1 quart beef, chicken, or vegetable stock, homemade (pages 18–22) or store-bought

3 cups water

1 (28-ounce) can diced tomatoes with juice, or 3 1/2 cups peeled and diced tomatoes

2 cups thinly sliced fresh, young okra or frozen okra pieces

1 1/2–2 cups cooked long-grain white rice, hot or warm, for serving

In a Dutch oven over medium-high heat, melt the butter and lard. Add the onion and parsley and gently cook until the onion is translucent and soft, about 5 minutes. Add the garlic and cook for 1 minute more, until fragrant. Add the thyme, salt, kitchen pepper, and red pepper flakes and cook for another minute or so. Add the stock, water, and tomatoes, turn the heat down to medium-low, and simmer for 30 minutes. Add the okra and cook for another 20–25 minutes, until the okra is tender.

To serve, place ¼ cup warm rice in each serving bowl and ladle the soup over the top.

Red Rice

This recipe for the Low Country classic was inspired by the erudite Damon Lee Fowler, culinary historian and cookbook author from Savannah and a keeper of old southern culinary traditions. This tomato pilau is one of the greatest dishes ever to emerge from the Low Country and can be adjusted depending on your tastes.

This recipe was published in Fowler's The Savannah Cookbook, *published in 2008 by Gibbs Smith, and is included here by permission.*

MAKES 4–6 SERVINGS

¼ pound thick-cut bacon or salt pork, diced small

1 medium onion, trimmed, split lengthwise, peeled, and chopped

1 medium green bell pepper, stemmed, seeded, and chopped

1 cup long-grain rice, washed and drained

2 cups Italian canned plum tomatoes, with their juice, chopped

1 cup beef or chicken stock, homemade (pages 18–20) or store-bought, or water

1 tablespoon Worcestershire sauce

Salt, ground cayenne pepper, and whole black pepper in a peppermill or Kitchen Pepper (page 16)

Put the bacon or salt pork in a Dutch oven and turn the heat to medium. Fry, uncovered, until the fat is rendered and the bacon is crisp. Spoon off all but 2 tablespoons of fat. Add the onion and bell pepper and sauté until translucent, about 5 minutes.

Add the rice and stir until it's well coated and warmed, about 3 or 4 minutes. Add the tomatoes with their juice, stock, Worcestershire sauce, salt, cayenne, and a liberal grinding of pepper to taste. Bring to a boil and stir, scraping any loose grains that are sticking to the pan.

Loosely cover, reduce the heat as low as possible, and let simmer for 25 minutes. Remove it from the heat and allow to steam for 15 minutes before serving.

Limpin' Susan

Okra and rice, a staple from the shores of West Africa to the shores of the American South. The two ingredients dance well together in this often-forgotten southern classic. The okra doesn't have to be slimy: make sure it's young, cut it small, and don't overcook it.

MAKES 4–6 SERVINGS

5 thick bacon slices
3 cups thinly sliced young okra
1 small yellow onion, minced
2 garlic cloves, peeled and smashed
1 cup long-grain white rice, washed and drained
1 cup vegetable stock, homemade (page 22) or store-bought
1 teaspoon kosher salt
½ teaspoon freshly ground black pepper or Kitchen Pepper
   (page 16)

In a Dutch oven over medium-high heat, fry the bacon until it's crisp and most of the fat is rendered. Using a slotted spoon, transfer the bacon to paper towels to drain, leaving the fat in the pot. Crumble the bacon and set aside.

Add the okra, onion, and garlic to the pot and sauté until the onion is translucent, about 5 minutes. Add the rice, stock, salt, and pepper, and turn the heat up to high to bring to a boil. Boil for 5 minutes, stirring occasionally to make sure that all of the ingredients are incorporated.

Turn the heat down to low and place a sheet of aluminum foil over the Dutch oven, then replace the lid. Simmer for 25 minutes, then remove the pot from the heat and let it sit, still covered, for 15 minutes. Add the crumbled bacon, stir gently, and serve hot.

Shrimp Rice

This dish, created by Chef BJ Dennis, is what happens when you are blessed to live in a community with fresh, sweet, plump shrimp full of brine and marine flavors. Shrimp rice is a simple way to celebrate the arrays of pink set off by the colors of the ingredients and the rice.

MAKES 4–6 SERVINGS

2 pounds raw whole (heads and tails on) medium shrimp, deveined but not peeled, or 1¼ pounds raw medium shrimp, heads removed, deveined but not peeled

¼ cup plus 1 tablespoon unsalted butter

½ cup finely chopped shallot (about 1 large or 2 medium) or red onion

1 large or 2 medium garlic cloves, peeled, lightly smashed, and minced

3 cups Southern Dry Rice (page 17)

Ground cayenne pepper, to taste

Kosher salt, to taste

Peel the shrimp and remove the heads, reserving both the heads and shells. Put the butter in a large, deep skillet or sauté pan over medium-high heat. When it's melted, add the shrimp heads and shells and sauté, tossing constantly, until the shells and butter are bright orange-pink and the butter is deeply infused with the essence of the shrimp. Strain the butter through a fine-mesh strainer into a bowl, pressing hard on the shells. Discard the shells and return the butter to the pan.

Add the shallot and sauté, tossing frequently, until they're softened and beginning to color, about 4 minutes. Add the garlic and peeled shrimp and sauté, tossing frequently, until the shrimp are curled and pink, about 2 minutes. Stir in the rice and cook, tossing constantly, until it's hot all the way through. Season well with cayenne and salt, toss well, and serve at once.

Oyster Pilau

A hearty winter dish from the South Carolina Low Country, oyster pilau is perfect for oyster lovers. It makes good use of all the coastal marsh and Sea Islands have to offer as the world goes gray and cold. Brine and sea get into your nostrils and your soul.

MAKES 4–6 SERVINGS

½ pound salt pork
1 pint fresh shucked oysters
¼ cup chopped green bell pepper
¼ cup diced yellow onion
½ teaspoon paprika
1 tablespoon Worcestershire sauce
2 teaspoons hot sauce
1 teaspoon kosher salt
2 cups long-grain white rice, washed and drained
2½ cups vegetable, chicken, or beef stock, homemade
   (pages 18–22) or store-bought

In a large Dutch oven over medium-high heat, fry the salt pork until golden brown. Add the oysters, then add the bell pepper, onion, paprika, Worcestershire sauce, hot sauce, and salt. Turn the heat down to medium and cook for a few minutes, until the oysters start to curl a bit.

Add the rice and stock, stir once or twice, and cover. Turn the heat down to low and simmer for 30–40 minutes, until the rice is tender and has absorbed all of the liquid. Serve immediately.

Pork Chops and Rice

This recipe elevates delicious pork chops by smothering them in a traditional highly seasoned, rich Creole sauce.

MAKES 4 SERVINGS

---

4 (1-inch-thick) bone-in pork loin chops
Seasoned salt
Freshly ground black pepper or Kitchen Pepper (page 16)
All-purpose flour, for dredging
1 tablespoon vegetable shortening
3 tablespoons vegetable oil
1 medium yellow onion, sliced
2 tomatoes, diced
1 green bell pepper, diced
½ cup long-grain white rice, washed and drained
2 cups beef stock, homemade (page 20) or store-bought

Preheat the oven to 375°. Sprinkle the pork chops all over with seasoned salt and pepper and dredge them in flour.

Melt the vegetable shortening and the vegetable oil together in a large heavy-bottomed skillet over medium-high heat and lightly fry the chops until they're brown on both sides, about 5–6 minutes per side. Transfer the chops to a shallow baking dish.

Place 2 slices of onion on each chop, then cover them with the diced tomato and bell pepper. Pour the rice between the chops, then add the stock . Cover with aluminum foil and bake for about 1 hour and 15 minutes, until the rice is tender. Halfway through cooking, add as much water or broth as you need to complete the cooking of the rice; the rice should be moist. Stir to mix everything together before serving.

Chicken and Rice

Chicken and rice is a basic perloo dish that takes different forms across the Carolinas and the Deep South. It was once one of the main staple dishes of large gatherings and Sunday dinners.

MAKES 8 SERVINGS

1 (6-pound) whole chicken
6 celery stalks
Kosher salt, to taste
Kitchen Pepper (page 16), to taste
Dash of ground cayenne pepper
2 cups vegetable or chicken stock, homemade (pages 18 and 22) or store-bought, plus more if needed
2½ cups converted rice

FOR THE GRAVY
3 tablespoons unsalted butter
3 tablespoons all-purpose flour
3½ cups cooking liquid, from above

Chopped fresh parsley, for garnish

Rinse the chicken and pat it dry. Place the chicken and celery in a large, heavy-bottomed pot with a tight-fitting lid and fill two-thirds full with stock. Add a little salt, kitchen pepper, and a dash of cayenne pepper. Cover and bring to a boil over high heat. Boil for 1 hour, then turn the heat down to low and simmer for 1½ hours, or until the chicken is tender and cooked through.

Remove the chicken from the pot and debone it. Set aside a few of the chicken pieces to top the finished dish. Discard the celery. Transfer 3½ cups of the cooking liquid from the pot to a bowl and set aside for making gravy. There should be about 3 cups of liquid left in the pot.

Place the deboned chicken meat in the pot. Add the rice and bring to a boil over high heat. Boil for 5 minutes, then turn the heat down to low, cover, and cook for 20–30 minutes, until the rice has absorbed all of the liquid. Taste and adjust the seasonings as desired.

For the gravy: Melt the butter in a saucepan over low heat, stir in the flour, and cook for 2 minutes, stirring constantly with a wooden spoon. Gradually add the reserved cooking liquid and simmer until thickened, 5–10 minutes.

To serve, spoon the chicken and rice onto a heated platter. Top with the reserved chicken pieces. Pour some of the gravy over the rice and serve the rest in a gravy boat. Sprinkle the dish with chopped parsley and serve immediately.

Country Captain à la Hazel

This is my Alabama grandmother's recipe for country captain, a southern curry-flavored rice dish popular in the Carolina Low Country and other parts of the Lower South. You can also taste the influence of West Africa, India, and Great Britain in the rural South all at once.

MAKES 6–8 SERVINGS

8 pieces skin-on, bone-in chicken (thighs, legs, drumsticks, breasts cut in half)

FOR THE CHICKEN RUB
1 tablespoon kosher salt
1 teaspoon ground cinnamon
1 teaspoon Kitchen Pepper (page 16)
1 teaspoon Madras curry powder
1 teaspoon poultry seasoning
1 teaspoon red pepper flakes

FOR THE COUNTRY CAPTAIN
3 cups basmati rice, washed and drained
¼ cup canola oil or bacon fat
1 green bell pepper, seeded and chopped
1 large red onion, chopped
4 garlic cloves, minced
1 tablespoon peeled and finely chopped fresh ginger
1 tablespoon Madras curry powder
2 teaspoons Kitchen Pepper (page 16)
1 teaspoon kosher salt
1 (28-ounce) can crushed tomatoes, with juice
1 (6-ounce) can tomato paste
4 cups no-salt-added vegetable stock, homemade (page 22) or store-bought

1 cup vegetable or canola oil, or $\frac{1}{2}$ cup vegetable or canola oil
   mixed with $\frac{1}{2}$ cup bacon fat
1 cup all-purpose flour

FOR GARNISH (OPTIONAL)
Carrot shavings
Chopped fresh parsley
Chopped tomatoes
Raisins
Sliced green onion
Slivered almonds
Unsweetened coconut flakes

Pat the chicken dry with a paper towel and place it in a large mixing bowl. Add the salt and seasonings and rub them all over the chicken, coating it well. Cover the bowl with plastic wrap and refrigerate for at least 3–4 hours, or preferably overnight.

When you're ready to begin cooking, place the rice in a large pot with a tight-fitting lid and add enough water to cover the rice by 1 inch. Cover and bring to a boil over medium-high heat, then turn the heat down to low and simmer, covered, until the rice is fluffy and the liquid has evaporated, about 20–25 minutes. Fluff the rice with a fork and then replace the lid to keep it warm. Set aside.

While the rice is cooking, in a large, heavy-bottomed pot with a tight-fitting lid, heat the canola oil over medium-high heat. Add the bell pepper, onion, garlic, and ginger. Sauté until the onion has softened and become translucent, about 5–8 minutes. Stir in the curry powder, kitchen pepper, and salt, then add the crushed tomatoes with juice and the tomato paste. Continue to cook, stirring constantly, for 3–4 minutes. Add the stock and bring it to a boil over high heat, then turn the heat down to low and simmer, uncovered, for 30 minutes. Taste and adjust the seasonings as needed.

While the sauce cooks, prepare the seasoned chicken for frying. In a large, heavy-bottomed pot, heat the vegetable oil over medium-high heat. The oil is hot enough when it can brown a cube of bread. Place the flour in a shallow bowl, dredge each piece of chicken in the flour, shake off the excess, and place the piece of chicken on a plate. Working in batches to avoid overcrowding the pan, shallow-fry the chicken for about 4–5 minutes per side, until the chicken is golden brown on both sides. As you finish each piece of chicken, place it on a plate lined with a paper towel.

Add the fried chicken to the pot of simmering sauce and bring it to a boil over medium-high heat, then turn the heat down to low. Cover and simmer for about 35 minutes to allow the chicken to finish cooking and the liquid to thicken into a stew. Turn off the heat and let the chicken rest for about 10–15 minutes. Serve with the rice and any or all of the suggested garnishes.

Rice Dressing

This is an excellent gluten-free alternative to southern cornbread dressing for holiday meals. It's perfect for stuffing in a Cornish hen or chicken, or even a double-thick pork chop.

MAKES 4–6 SERVINGS

- 1 quart chicken stock, homemade (page 18) or store-bought, divided
- 1½ cups long-grain white rice, washed and drained
- ½ cup unsalted butter, cubed
- 2 cups chopped celery
- 2 cups chopped yellow onion
- 1 cup button mushrooms
- 3 tablespoons minced fresh parsley
- 1½–2 teaspoons poultry seasoning
- ¾ teaspoon seasoned salt
- ½ teaspoon freshly ground black pepper
- Chopped fresh sage (optional)
- Chopped fresh thyme leaves (optional)

Preheat the oven to 350° and grease a 9-by-13-inch baking dish.

In a saucepan with a tight-fitting lid, combine 3½ cups of the stock and the rice and bring to a boil over high heat. Turn the heat down to low, cover, and simmer until the rice is tender, about 20 minutes.

Melt the butter in a large skillet over medium-high heat. Add the celery and onion and sauté until tender, about 5 minutes. Stir in the cooked rice, mushrooms, parsley, poultry seasoning, seasoned salt, pepper, sage (if using), thyme (if using), and the remaining ½ cup of stock. Pour the rice mixture into the prepared baking dish. Bake, uncovered, for 30 minutes.

Sausage Pilau

This dish is inspired by a recipe recorded by Annabella Powell Dawson Hill, a resident of north Georgia in the nineteenth century. She published a cookbook called Mrs. Hill's New Cookbook *that is an extensive record of the cuisine of the Georgia Piedmont in the mid-to-late nineteenth century. We have Damon Lee Fowler to thank for uncovering much of her story.*

MAKES 4 SERVINGS

1½ pounds bulk pork sausage, formed into 1-inch balls
1 medium yellow onion, diced
1¾ cups vegetable or beef stock, homemade (pages 20–22)
    or store-bought
3 sprigs fresh thyme
2 bay leaves, fresh if possible
Kosher salt and freshly ground black pepper or Kitchen
    Pepper (page 16), to taste
Pinch of ground cayenne pepper, or to taste
1 cup long-grain white rice, washed and drained

Place the sausage balls in a large saucepan with a tight-fitting lid or Dutch oven over medium heat. Brown them well on all sides, being careful not to let them scorch. Drain off all but 2 tablespoons of the fat, add the onion, and sauté until it's translucent, about 5 minutes. Add the stock and bring to a boil, still over medium heat, then add the thyme and bay leaves. Turn the heat down to low, cover, and simmer for 30 minutes.

Taste the broth and season it with salt, pepper, and cayenne. Turn the heat to high, bring the broth to a boil, and add the rice. Stir and let the broth come back to a boil. Turn the heat down to low, cover, and simmer for 15–20 minutes. Turn off the heat and let the pan sit, still covered, for another 15 minutes. Fluff the rice with a fork and serve hot.

Crab Fried Rice

This is southern fried rice at its absolute best. It's also a great way to use up any leftover crab before it can go bad or lose its peak flavor.

MAKES 4 SERVINGS

---

4 thick-cut bacon slices, diced

1 green bell pepper, seeded and chopped

1 medium yellow onion, chopped

1 celery stalk, chopped

1 large or 2 medium garlic cloves, peeled, lightly smashed, and minced

1 pound crabmeat

3 cups Southern Dry Rice (page 17)

1 teaspoon kosher salt, or more to taste (see Note)

1 teaspoon freshly ground black pepper, or more to taste (see Note)

Put the bacon in a large, deep skillet or sauté pan with a tight-fitting lid over medium-high heat. Sauté, tossing frequently, until the bacon is crisp and the fat is rendered. Add the bell pepper, onion, and celery and sauté, tossing frequently, until the veggies are softened and the onion is golden, about 5 minutes. Add the garlic and crabmeat and sauté, tossing, until the crab is hot all the way through and lightly brown, about 5 minutes.

Add the rice and toss it until it's well-coated and the crab is evenly distributed. Season the mixture liberally with salt and pepper or crab boil seasoning. Toss well, turn the heat down to medium-low, cover, and let the rice steam gently for about 10 minutes. Taste and adjust the seasonings as desired. Toss well and serve hot.

NOTE ❋ In place of the salt and pepper, you can use 1 teaspoon finely ground crab boil seasoning, or more to taste.

Carolina Pilau

This is my rather elaborate version of a Low Country classic. It's just the trinity of peppers, tomatoes, and onions with all the chicken flavor we can muster, but the rich broth and Kitchen Pepper (page 16) elevate its taste and aroma.

MAKES 6–8 SERVINGS

1 (3½-to-4-pound) whole chicken

2 quarts chicken or vegetable stock, homemade (pages 18 and 22) or store-bought, or more if needed

½ cup (1 stick) unsalted butter

1 large yellow onion, chopped (about 1½ cups)

1½ cups chopped green bell pepper

1½ cups diced celery

2–3 large tomatoes (about 1 pound), peeled and chopped, with juice

1 tablespoon chopped fresh thyme leaves, or 1 teaspoon dried thyme leaves

1 teaspoon kosher salt

½ teaspoon freshly ground black pepper or Kitchen Pepper (page 16)

½ teaspoon red pepper flakes, or a dash of hot sauce

2 cups long-grain white rice, washed and drained

Place the chicken in a large pot and add enough stock to cover the chicken completely. Bring to a boil over medium heat and boil, uncovered, for 50 minutes, or until the chicken is cooked through (the internal temperature should reach 165°). Transfer the chicken from the broth to a cutting board and reserve the broth to use later. Remove the chicken skin and pull the meat from the bones. Cut the meat into uniform bite-size pieces. Set aside.

Melt the butter in a Dutch oven over medium heat, then add the onion, bell pepper, and the celery and cook until the onion starts to brown, about 10 minutes. Add the tomatoes with their juice and the seasonings. Add the chicken meat, the rice, and 1 quart of the reserved broth.

Bring to a boil, then cover and turn the heat down to low. Simmer slowly, without lifting the lid, for 30 minutes.

Shrimp Pilau

Remember, "pilau" = "perloo." This dish is the king of the Low Country shrimp season, a cousin to New Orleans shrimp Creole and a step up from shrimp and rice, thanks to all of the vegetable stars.

MAKES 4–6 SERVINGS

4 thick bacon slices

1 large yellow onion, diced

4 plump, overripe heirloom or plum tomatoes, peeled, seeded, and chopped

1 green bell pepper, seeded and diced

3 tablespoons chopped fresh parsley, plus more for garnish

Large pinch of ground cayenne pepper

1 teaspoon seasoned salt, Bay seasoning, or Creole seasoning

2 cups long-grain white rice, washed and drained

3 cups shrimp stock or vegetable stock, homemade (page 22) or store-bought

1½ pounds cooked medium shrimp, peeled and deveined, heads and tails removed

In a Dutch oven with a tight-fitting lid, cook the bacon over high heat until it's crisp. Using a slotted spoon, remove the bacon from the pan and set it on paper towels to drain, leaving the fat in the pan. Pour off all of the bacon fat but about 3 tablespoons, enough to cover the bottom of the pan.

Turn the heat down to medium-low, add the onion, and cook for 5–10 minutes, until transparent. Add the tomatoes, bell pepper, parsley, and ground cayenne pepper and cook for another 5 minutes. Add the seasoned salt, then add the rice and stock and stir to combine. Increase the heat to high for 1–2 minutes and bring to a simmer. Turn the heat back down to low, cover the pot, and simmer for 20 minutes without lifting the lid.

Fluff the rice with a big fork and toss in the shrimp. Cover the pot again, remove it from the heat, and let it sit for 15 minutes. Crumble the reserved bacon and garnish the pilau with it and some chopped parsley.

Dirty Rice

This is a Louisiana staple that makes use of leftovers and ingredients that would always be on hand in a Lower Mississippi River valley kitchen. Again, rice's versatility and economy are alive and on display.

MAKES 6–8 SERVINGS

½ pound chicken gizzards, coarsely chopped

½ pound chicken livers, coarsely chopped

2 medium yellow onions, diced

1 large green bell pepper, seeded and chopped

½ cup coarsely chopped celery

2 tablespoons extra-virgin olive oil

1½ teaspoons Creole seasoning

½ teaspoon freshly ground black pepper or Kitchen Pepper (page 16)

2 tablespoons Worcestershire sauce

1 tablespoon hot sauce

1 recipe Southern Dry Rice (page 17) (see Note)

½ cup finely chopped fresh flat-leaf parsley, for garnish

Purée the chicken gizzards, livers, onions, bell pepper, and celery in a food processor until chunky. In a large pot, heat the olive oil over medium heat. Add the gizzard-and-liver mixture, stir in the Creole seasoning, pepper, Worcestershire, and hot sauce, and turn the heat down to low. Cook, uncovered, until the bits of chicken are richly browned, about 1 hour, stirring occasionally.

Carefully add the rice to the gizzard-and-liver mixture and stir to combine. Garnish with parsley and serve immediately.

NOTE ❋ Make sure you don't use converted rice for this recipe.

Hoppin' John

This classic rice-and-peas dish came directly from West Africa and spread across the American South. It was known as jambalaya au congri in Louisiana. Eat a bit on New Year's for good luck and for change in your wallet and change in your life!

MAKES 4–6 SERVINGS

---

1 ham knuckle, or ¼ pound dried salt pork (need not be precooked), diced (optional)

1 green bell pepper, seeded and diced

1 medium yellow or red onion, diced

1 quart low-sodium beef, chicken, or vegetable stock, homemade (pages 18–22) or store-bought

1 cup dried black-eyed peas, soaked in water overnight and drained

1 recipe Southern Dry Rice (page 17)

1 tablespoon unsalted butter

Pinch of ground cayenne pepper

1 teaspoon kosher salt

½ teaspoon freshly ground black pepper or Kitchen Pepper (page 16)

Place the ham knuckle (if using) in a pot with a tight-fitting lid and add the green pepper, onion, and stock. Make sure the stock covers the ingredients by 1 inch. Cover and bring to a boil over high heat, then immediately turn the heat down to low and simmer for 2 hours. Add the black-eyed peas and simmer until they're tender, 1 hour or so.

When the peas are done, add the rice, butter, cayenne, and salt and pepper. Cook over low heat until all of the liquid is absorbed, about 15–20 minutes.

Breads and Desserts

Rice isn't just a side dish or a base for an entrée. In the American South, it's also breakfast, dessert, and a snack. Rice partners well with vanilla, sweet spices, and even cane syrup, which brings out its creamier elements. For those who have not previously made bread and desserts with rice, here we introduce a few age-old rice confections and delicious baked goods that provide traditional alternatives to wheat-based foods.

Nancie's Historic Rice Pudding

Rice pudding recipes from eighteenth-century southern kitchens reflect British colonial heritage and are made with common modern ingredients: milk, butter, and eggs. Some also feature specialty ingredients, such as rose water or orange flower water, grated lemon or orange peel, or wine. Some early recipes call for baking rice pudding in a crust, making it a pie by modern definition. This is Nancie McDermott's updated version of an eighteenth-century recipe.

MAKES 4–6 SERVINGS

- ¾ cup long-grain white rice, washed and drained
- Pinch of kosher salt
- 3 cups whole milk
- ½ cup packed light or dark brown sugar
- 1 teaspoon grated lemon peel
- ½ teaspoon freshly grated nutmeg
- 3 tablespoons unsalted butter, cut into small pieces
- 3 large eggs, beaten well
- ½ cup currants or raisins

Preheat the oven to 375°.

In a medium saucepan with a tight-fitting lid, combine the rice and salt, then add enough water to cover the rice by 1 inch. Place the pan over medium-high heat, stir well, and bring it to a lively boil, stirring occasionally. While the rice comes to a boil, generously grease a 9-by-13-inch baking pan with butter, shortening, or vegetable oil.

When the rice is boiling, turn the heat down to medium-low to maintain a gentle but visible boil. Cook uncovered until the water level drops and the rice begins to swell, about 3–5 minutes, then cover and turn the heat down to low. Cook undisturbed for 15 minutes, then remove the pan from the heat.

While the rice cooks, combine the milk, brown sugar, lemon peel, and nutmeg in a large mixing bowl. Use a whisk or a fork to combine everything well.

When the rice has cooked for 15 minutes, stir well, fluffing up the rice from the bottom of the pot. Add the butter and stir to melt it completely in the hot rice. Transfer the hot, buttery rice to the bowl of milk and stir it gently with a large spoon or spatula to combine the rice and the milk mixture.

Add the beaten eggs and currants and stir to mix everything together evenly. Pour the rice pudding into the prepared baking pan and bake until the pudding has set into a fairly firm custard and the top is dry and handsomely browned, 45–55 minutes. A toothpick inserted into the center of the pudding should come out clean.

Place the baking dish on a wire cooling rack or folded kitchen towels to cool. Serve warm or at room temperature.

Savannah Rice Waffles

The perfect companion for chicken Madeira and other fancy and delicious braises, this gem is another recipe generously contributed by Savannah's culinary scholar Damon Lee Fowler. This recipe was published in Fowler's The Savannah Cookbook, *published in 2008 by Gibbs Smith, and is included here by permission.*

MAKES ABOUT 6 LARGE OR 10–12 SMALL WAFFLES

2 tablespoons unsalted butter

1 cup hot, steamed rice

10 ounces (about 2 cups) unbleached all-purpose flour

2 teaspoons baking powder

$\frac{1}{2}$ teaspoon baking soda

1 teaspoon salt

2 large eggs, separated

1$\frac{3}{4}$ cups whole-milk buttermilk or plain, whole-milk yogurt
    thinned to buttermilk consistency with milk

Melted butter or oil, for greasing the waffle iron

Stir the butter into the hot rice until melted and incorporated, then let it cool to room temperature.

Meanwhile, whisk or sift together the flour, baking powder, baking soda, and salt in a mixing bowl and make a well in the center. Beat the egg yolks and buttermilk together and pour them into the flour. Quickly mix the wet and dry ingredients together and stir in the rice.

Prepare a waffle iron and preheat at medium. In a separate bowl, beat the egg whites until they form soft peaks. When the iron is ready, fold the egg whites into the batter, brush the iron well with fat, and spoon some of the batter evenly over it, leaving room at the edges for it to spread as it cooks. Close the iron and bake until the steam stops rising from it and the waffle smells toasty and is golden brown, about 5–8 minutes. Serve the waffles as soon as they come off the iron and repeat with the remaining batter.

Rice Bread

Another recipe generously shared by South Carolina's own John Martin Taylor, whose work is indispensable to understanding the southern rice kitchen. Southern rice breads owed a lot to the meeting of English baking traditions with those from the Rice Coast of West Africa. To the point, this recipe is reminiscent of the Liberian Rice Bread on page 29, minus the more dessert-like elements. This recipe makes a large quantity, suitable for serving at a party, buffet, or reception.

MAKES THREE 8½-BY-4½-INCH LOAVES

1 pound long-grain white rice (about 2½ cups)
3 tablespoons kosher salt
¾ ounces active instant dry yeast
4 pounds unbleached bread flour (about 14½ cups)

Place the rice and salt in a large pot and add enough water to cover the rice by 1 inch. Set over high heat and boil, uncovered, until all of the liquid is absorbed and the rice is soft, about 20–30 minutes.

Divide the cooked rice between two large bowls and set them aside to cool. When the rice is cool enough to handle, divide the yeast between the bowls and stir to mix it into the rice, then divide the flour between the bowls and work it into the rice, kneading and folding it all together in the bowls until you have a smooth, elastic loaf, about 10 minutes.

Wipe the rim of the bowls clean, then cover them tightly with plastic wrap. If your bowls aren't large enough to allow the bread to double in size, brush the top of the dough with oil or butter to keep it from sticking to the plastic. Cover each plastic-wrapped bowl with a towel and set it in a warm place to rise for about 2 hours.

Grease three 8½-by-4½-inch loaf pans and set them aside. When the dough has doubled, punch it down, knead it lightly, and set it on a lightly floured work surface. Divide the dough into three parts and roll each part into a log that fits into a loaf pan, with all edges on the bottom and only the smooth top showing. Cover each loaf pan with plastic wrap and a towel and place them on top of the stove. Preheat the oven to 450°. Check the loaves at 30 minutes; they should have risen to the tops of the pans by then.

Remove the towels and plastic wrap and set the loaf pans in the preheated oven. Bake for 15 minutes at 450°, then turn the oven down to 400° and bake for another 15 minutes.

Remove the pans from the oven and unpan the loaves. Set the loaves directly on the oven rack and bake for 15–25 minutes more, until the loaves are golden brown and a toothpick inserted in the center comes out clean. If the loaves seem to be browning too quickly, turn the oven down to 350°. Watch the loaves to ensure that they brown evenly. Transfer to wire cooling racks to cool.

Store in a cool, dry location. Best eaten within 2 days.

Princess Pamela's Rice Fritters

Princess Pamela Strobel was a South Carolina chef who ran a successful restaurant in New York from the 1960s to the 1990s and published an incredible cookbook that was revised and revived in 2017. These rice fritters were once common throughout the South and use leftover rice to make a treat that kids of all ages will enjoy.

This recipe was published in Pamela Strobel's Princess Pamela's Soul Food Cookbook, *published in 2017 by Rizzoli International Publications, and is included here by permission.*

MAKES 6 SERVINGS

1 cup all purpose flour
1 cup sugar
2 teaspoons baking powder
A pinch of salt
2 eggs, separated
1 cup cold cooked, slightly mashed long-grain rice
$\frac{1}{8}$ teaspoon cinnamon or nutmeg

Sift together the flour, sugar, baking powder, and salt. Beat the egg yolks until they're thick. Stir in the flour mixture, rice, and cinnamon. Beat the egg whites until they're stiff and fold them into the rice mixture. Drop them from a tablespoon into deep, hot oil and fry them for 2-3 minutes or until they're golden brown. Drain the fritters on paper towels and serve hot, with cane syrup or sorghum molasses, or sprinkled with powdered sugar.

NOTE ❋ When I've cooked these in my kitchen, this is how I fry them: Pour the oil into a large Dutch oven to a depth of about 3 inches. Place the pot over high heat and heat the oil to 350°. When the end of a wooden spoon sizzles when dipped into the oil, it's ready. Drop the dough by the tablespoon into the oil and deep-fry them over medium-high heat, two or three at a time, turning them frequently with a slotted spoon. As they turn golden brown, use the slotted spoon to transfer them to paper towels to drain.

Philpy

I learned about this classic southern rice bread through the scholarship of my friend John Martin Taylor, who has worked extensively with old southern receipt (an old term for "recipe") records. This recipe owes much to his expertise in reinvigorating the southern culinary past.

MAKES ONE 8-INCH PHILPY (8 SERVINGS)

Bacon fat
½ cup soft-cooked long-grain white rice, cooled
½ cup rice flour
¼ cup plus 2 tablespoons water
1 large egg, lightly beaten
¼ teaspoon kosher salt (optional)
Butter, for serving

Thoroughly grease an 8-inch pie plate or small cast-iron skillet with bacon fat. Place it in a cold oven, then set the oven to 425°. The pan will heat while you make the batter.

Rub the rice through a sieve into a medium mixing bowl. In a separate mixing bowl, mix the rice flour and water into a smooth paste, then add it to the rice. Add the egg and stir until all the ingredients are well combined. If the rice was cooked with salt, add none to the batter; otherwise, add the salt and stir.

Fold the batter into the hot pan. Bake until golden, about 30 minutes. Immediately, without waiting for it to cool, cut it into 8 slices, butter the slices, and serve.

Sugar and Rice

A popular folk breakfast from the South, sugar and rice brings back for many fond memories of childhood and making do with what you have.

MAKES 2–3 SERVINGS

1 cup water
2 tablespoons unsalted butter, divided
1½ cups cooked short-grain white rice
¼ cup white or light brown sugar
¼ cup whole milk, warm
Pinch of ground cinnamon or freshly grated nutmeg,
    for garnish (optional)

Place the water and 1 tablespoon of the butter in a medium saucepan with a tight-fitting lid and bring to a boil over high heat. Add the cooked rice and stir, then immediately remove the pan from the heat, cover, and let it sit for 5 minutes.

Add the sugar and the remaining tablespoon of butter, and stir to combine. Transfer the rice to your favorite cereal bowls, stir in the warm milk, and sprinkle with cinnamon if desired before serving.

Louisiana Calas

Calas are a form of akara, a type of deep-fried fritter from West Africa that is most often made with black-eyed peas but can also be made with rice, millet, and other grains. Calas are most closely associated with Louisiana, however; they were sold on the streets of antebellum New Orleans by Black Creole ladies. They are tasty and must be served piping hot.

MAKES 6 CALAS (3–4 SERVINGS)

1½ cups water

⅔ cup long-grain white rice (not converted), washed and drained

1½ cups all-purpose flour

1½ teaspoons double-acting baking powder

½ teaspoon ground cinnamon

½ teaspoon freshly grated nutmeg

Pinch of kosher salt

2 large eggs

2 tablespoons sugar

Vegetable oil, for deep frying

Cane syrup, for serving (optional)

Powdered sugar, for topping (optional)

Bring the water to a boil in a small, heavy-bottomed saucepan with a tight-fitting lid. Slowly pour in the rice and stir two or three times. Add more water if necessary to cover the rice by 1 inch, then cover the pan tightly. Turn the heat down to low and simmer for 20 minutes, or until the rice has absorbed all of the liquid. Remove the pan from the heat and let it sit, still covered, for another 15 minutes to ensure maximum water absorption. Spread the cooked rice out in a large skillet and allow it to cool to room temperature.

Whisk or sift together the flour, baking powder, spices, and salt into a medium mixing bowl. Set aside.

In a large mixing bowl, beat the eggs and sugar for several minutes until sugar is dissolved. Add the cooled rice and stir with a spoon until the rice is well coated. Add the dry ingredients to the rice-and-eggs mixture ½ cup at a time, stirring constantly, until well mixed and a dough forms.

Place the rice dough on a lightly floured work surface and divide it into six even portions. Moistening your hands frequently with cold water to prevent sticking, shape each portion into a ball. They should each be the size of a golf ball.

Pour the oil into a large Dutch oven to a depth of about 3 inches. Place the pot over high heat and heat the oil to 350°. When the end of a wooden spoon sizzles when dipped into the oil, it's ready. Deep-fry the calas over medium-high heat, two or three at a time, turning them frequently with a slotted spoon. As they turn golden brown, use the slotted spoon to transfer them to paper towels to drain. Have your cane syrup and powdered sugar ready and serve the calas piping hot! They must be eaten hot and fresh.

Index